101
WING-T FROM A TO Z
PLAYS

DENNIS CREEHAN

ISBN: 978-1-58518-594-8
Library of Congress Control Number: 2001098604
Book layout and cover design: Rebecca Gold Rubin

Coaches Choice
PO Box 1828
Monterey, CA 93942
www.coacheschoice.com

CONTENTS

Preface 5

Chapter 1. The Sweep Series 7

Chapter 2. The Power Series 29

Chapter 3. The Trap Option Series 35

Chapter 4. The Down Series 51

Chapter 5. The Belly Cross Block Series 63

Chapter 6. The Quick Belly Series 101

About the Author 115

This book was compiled as a complement to the two-volume series of books entitled, *The Wing T from A to Z*. Similar to the two other books on the wing-T, it was written to help those coaches who are installing or currently running this great offense. While it would be almost impossible to put every single possible play that can be employed in this offensive scheme on paper, this book is designed to provide coaches at all competitive levels with 101 of the more commonly run and time-tested plays that have been employed over the years in the wing-T offense.

My sincere advice to every coach who reads this book is to package your plays and not "grab-bag" them. Be a purist for best results! Keep in mind that, one complete package is better than bits and pieces. It is my sincere wish that you have as much success and enjoyment running this offense as I have enjoyed over the years.

CHAPTER 1

THE
SWEEP SERIES

PLAY #1: 121

Use this sweep play when the wing back can block the end man on the line of scrimmage. Do not run this play when the end man is penetrating.

Blocking Rules:

TE – Gap; read down

RT – Gap; read down

RG – Pull; kick out

C – Reach; area away

LG – Pull; wall off

LT – Cutoff

SE – Out route

Backfield Coaching Points:

QB – Reverse pivot to midline; hand off to LH; fake waggle

LH – Carrier; stay tight to RH's down block

FB – Dive for left foot of OC; block area

RH – Block first free man inside

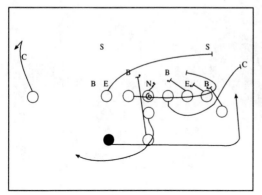

Vs. 5-0

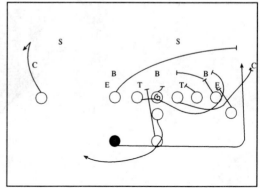

Vs. 4-3

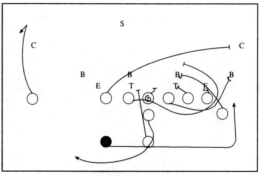

Vs. 4-4

PLAY #2: RIGHT 121

Run this sweep when you want to remove the corner and add extra blocking strength at the point of attack. If the defense overshifts to the strength, then run your attack to the weakside.

Blocking:

TE – Gap; read down

RT – Gap; read down

RG – Pull; kick out

C – Reach; area away

LG – Pull; wall off

LT – Cutoff

SE – Stalk corner

Backfield Coaching Points:

QB – Reverse pivot to midline; handoff to LH; fake waggle

LH – Carrier; stay tight to RH's down block

FB – Dive for left foot of OC; block area

RH – Block first free man inside

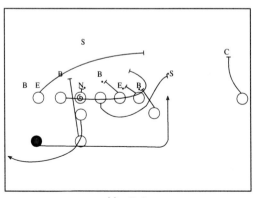

Vs. 5-0

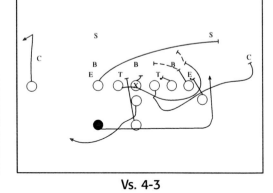

Vs. 4-3

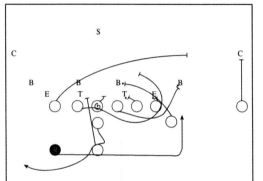

Vs. 4-4

This play could be run from LNB.

PLAY #3: SPLIT 129

Run this weakside sweep when the defense overshifts to the tight-end side. Run this in combination with the belly cross block to the weakside.

Blocking Rules:

SE – Down; backer

LT – Gap; read down

LG – Pull; kick out

OC – Reach; area away

RG – Pull; wall off

RT – Cutoff

TE – Cutoff

Backfield Coaching Points:

QB – Reverse pivot to midline; hand off to RH; fake waggle

LH – Go for a point 1.5 yards outside LT; block 1st free man inside

FB – Dive for right foot of OC; block area

RH – 3-step motion; carrier; stay tight to SE's block

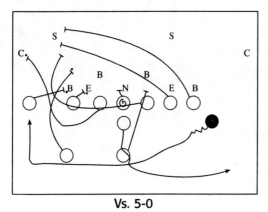

Vs. 5-0

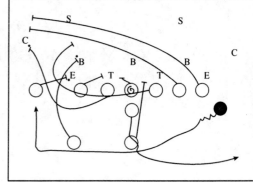

Vs. 4-3

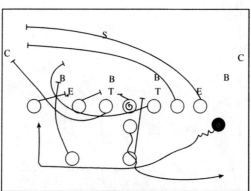

Vs. 4-4

PLAY #4: TIGHT 129

Run this sweep on the goal line if the end man on the line of scrimmage is not penetrating.

Blocking Rules:

LE – Gap; read down

LT – Gap; read down

LG – Pull; kick out

C – Reach; area away

RG – Pull; wall off

RT – Cutoff

TE – Cutoff

Backfield Coaching Points:

QB – Reverse pivot to midline; hand off to RH; fake waggle

LH – Go for a point 1.5 yards outside LE; block first free man inside

FB – Dive for right foot of OC; block area

RH – 3-step motion; carrier; stay tight to LH's block

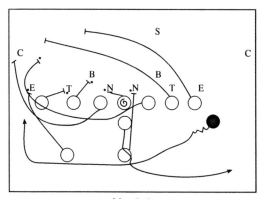

Vs. 6-2

This is a goal line play, but it can be run vs. any defense.

Play #5: 122 GUT

Run this play when the end man on the line of scrimmage is penetrating or working out to stop the sweep.

Blocking Rules:

TE – Gap; read down

RT – Gap; read down

RG – Pull; wall off

C – Reach; area away

LG – Pull; kick out

LT – Cutoff

SE – Out route

Backfield Coaching Points:

QB – Reverse pivot to midline; hand off to LH; fake waggle

LH – Carrier; bend path for off– tackle area

FB – Dive for left foot of OC; block area

RH – Influence end man on L.O.S.; block outside area

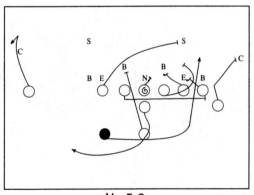

Vs. 5-0

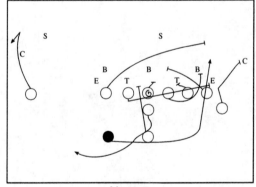

Vs. 4-3

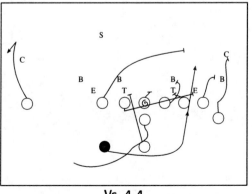

Vs. 4-4

PLAY #6: 122 POWER

Run this play when the end man on the line of scrimmage is penetrating to stop the sweep, and the linebackers are keying the guards.

Blocking Rules:

TE – Lead; backer; influence

RT – Gap; post; lead; backer

RG – Gap; area; post

C – Reach; area; away

LG – Pull; kick out

LT – Fire on; backer

SE – Out route

Backfield Coaching Points:

QB – Reverse pivot to midline; hand off to LH; fake waggle

LH – Carrier; bend path for off—tackle area

FB – Dive for left foot of OC; block area

RH – Influence end man on L.O.S.; block outside area

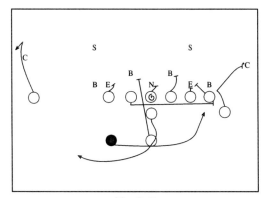

Vs. 5-0

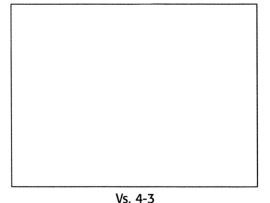

Vs. 4-3

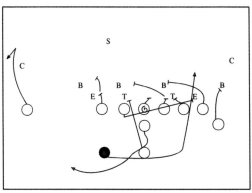

Vs. 4-4

PLAY #7: 122 TAG

Run this play vs. even defenses when the end man on the line of scrimmage is penetrating or working out to stop the sweep.

Blocking Rules:

TE – Lead; backer; influence

RT – Gap; post; lead; backer

RG – Gap; area; post

C – On; left

LG – Pull; kick out

LT – Pull; wall off

SE – Out route

Backfield Coaching Points:

QB – Reverse pivot to midline; hand off to LH; fake waggle

LH – Carrier; bend path for off–tackle area

FB – Dive for left foot of LG; block area

RH – Influence end man on L.O.S.; block outside area

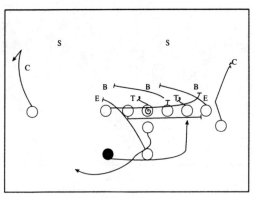

Vs. 4-3

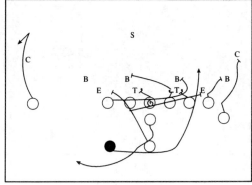

Vs. 4-4

PLAY #8: 124 GUARD TRAP

Run this play when the inside linebackers are running outside to stop the sweep and when the defensive linemen are not sealing down with the offensive tackles.

Blocking Rules:

TE – Backer; cutoff

RT – First backer from 5

RG – Lead; backer; influence

C – Post, left

LG – Pull; trap

LT – Block second man

SE – Out route

Backfield Coaching Points:

QB – Reverse pivot to midline
(over midline vs. odd); hand
off to FB, fake waggle

LH – Fake 21 sweep

FB – Carrier; stay tight to RG's
block

RH – Cutoff

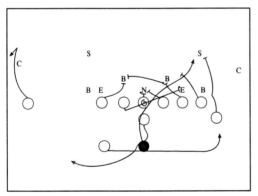

Vs. 5-0

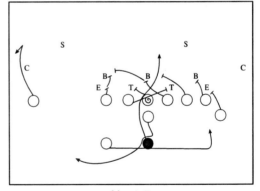

Vs. 4-3

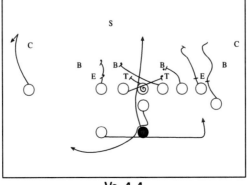

Vs. 4-4

PLAY #9: 124 GUARD TRAP GUT

Run this play if the defensive linemen are sealing down inside with the offensive tackles to stop the regular guard trap.

Blocking Rules:

TE – Gap; on; backer

RT – Gap; on; backer

RG – Gap; post; head; backer

C – Post; left

LG – Pull; gut

LT – Block second man

SE – Out route

Backfield Coaching Points:

QB – Reverse pivot to midline (over midline vs. odd); hand off to FB; fake waggle

LH – Fake 21 sweep

FB – Carrier; stay tight to RG's block

RH – Cutoff

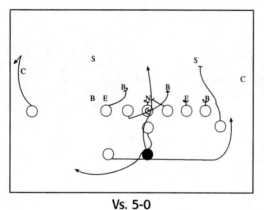

Vs. 5-0

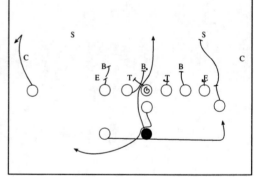

Vs. 4-3

Vs. 4-4

PLAY #10: 124 ON

Run this play vs. a team that plays a straight seven-man front. Also run this play if the defense is keying the guards.

Blocking Rules:

TE – Gap; on; backer

RT – Gap; on; backer

RG – Gap; on backer

C – On; backer

LG – Gap; on; backer

LT – Gap; on; backer

SE – Out route

Backfield Coaching Points:

QB – Reverse pivot to midline (over midline vs. odd); hand off to FB; fake waggle

LH – Fake 21 sweep

FB – Carrier; stay tight to OC's block; break off OC's block

RH – Cutoff

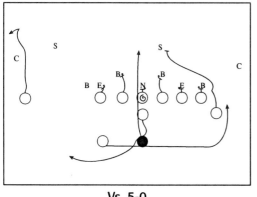

Vs. 5-0

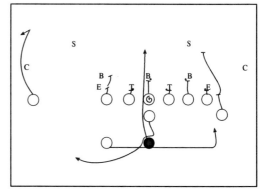

Vs. 4-3

We only run this play vs. 7-man front defenses.

PLAY #11: 124 ODD

Run this play when the defense is playing inside shades on the offensive tackles. It is also good if the defense is keying the guards.

Blocking Rules:

TE – Gap; on; backer

RT – Pull; gut for ILB

RG – On; outside

C – On; backer

LG – On; outside

LT – Pull; gut for ILB

SE – Out route

Backfield Coaching Points:

QB – Reverse pivot to midline
  (over midline vs. odd); hand
  off to FB; fake waggle

LH – Fake 21 sweep

FB – Carrier; stay tight to OC's
  block; break off OC's block

RH – Cutoff

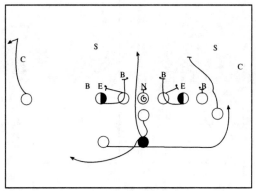

Vs. 5-0

We only run this play vs. a 5-0 defense.

PLAY #12: 124 GUARDS AWAY

Run this play only against an odd defense when it is absolutely certain that the linebackers are running with the guards.

Blocking Rules:

TE – Backer; cutoff

RT – On; outside

RG – Pull; kick out

C – On; backer

LG – Pull; kick out

LT – On; outside

SE – Out route

Backfield Coaching Points:

QB – Reverse pivot to midline (over midline vs. odd); hand off to FB; fake waggle

LH – Fake 21 sweep

FB – Carrier; stay tight to OC's block; break off OC's block

RH – Cutoff

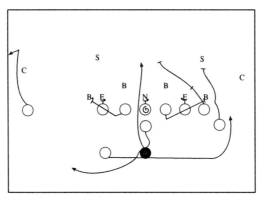

Vs. 5-0

We only run this play vs. a 5-0 defense.

PLAY #13: TIGHT 924 QB SNEAK

This is a goal-line play which should only be called for one yard or less. The offensive line uses wedge blocking, while the backs block out on the first man outside the blocks of the tight ends.

Blocking Rules:

RE – Gap; on; backer

RT – Gap; on backer

RG – Gap; on backer

C – Fire on; backer

LG – Fire on; backer

LT – Fire on; backer

LE – Fire on; backer

Backfield Coaching Points:

QB – Reverse pivot to midline;
   (over midline vs. odd); hand
   off to FB; fake waggle

LH – 3-step motion; fake 21
   sweep

FB – Dive for left foot on LT; block
   first man outside LE's block

RH – Dive for outside foot of RT;
   block first man outside RE's block

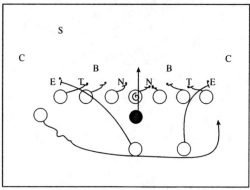

Vs. 6-2

Run this play vs. any defense, it is blocked the same way.

PLAY #14: 121 WAGGLE

Use this play when the defense over reacts to the sweep. Do not run this play if the end man on the line of scrimmage to the weakside is penetrating. If this play is run into edge pressure, the backside guard should kick out the edge pressure, and the QB should step up under the kickout.

Blocking Rules:

TE – Crossing route

RT – Pull; check 2

RG – Pull; read LG's block

OC – Block 1; cup right

LG – Pull; log end man

LT – Gap, down, on

SE – Fly route (individual cuts if called)

Backfield Coaching Points:

QB – Reverse pivot to midline; fake to LH; run pass option at flank

LH – Fake 21 sweep; block first man outside RT's block

FB – Dive for left foot of OC; block area; slide to flat

RH – Fake sweep block; run fly route

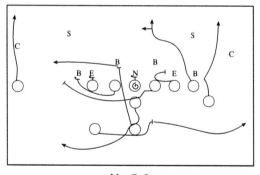

Vs. 5-0

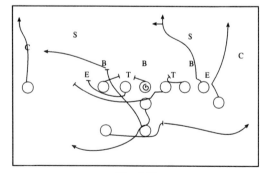

Vs. 4-3

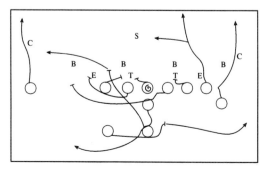

Vs. 4-4

PLAY #15: 121 WAGGLE SOLID

Use vs. a team that likes two-deep coverage and likes to support the sweep hard with their corners.

Blocking Rules:

RE – Fly route (inside SS)

RT – Step and cup

RG – Step and cup (pull vs. even)

C – On; right

LG –   Gap; on; pull

LT – Gap; on; area

SE – Fly route

Backfield Coaching Points:

QB – Reverse pivot to midline;
   fake to LH; pull up in G-T seam

LH – Fake 21 sweep; block first
   man outside Rt's block

FB – Dive for left foot on OC;
   block area

RH – Fake sweep block; run fly
   route; block first man outside

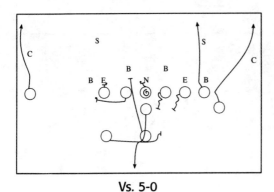

Vs. 5-0

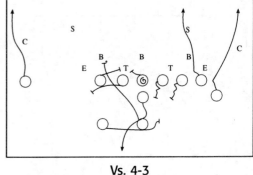

Vs. 4-3

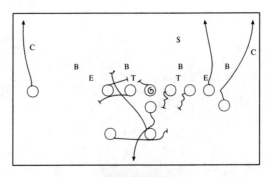

Vs. 4-4

PLAY #16: 121 WAGGLE SCREEN RIGHT

Use vs. a defense that chases hard off the backside trying to pressure the QB from behind.

Blocking Rules:

TE – Crossing route

RT – Pull; check 2; kick out

RG – Pull; read LG's block

OC – Block 1; cup right; wall off

LG – Pull; log end man

LT – Gap; down; on

SE – Fly route

Backfield Coaching Points:

QB – Reverse pivot to midline; fake to LH; pull up; throw screen to LH

LH – Fake 21 sweep; block first man outside RT's block; receive screen

FB – Dive for left foot of OC; block area; slide to flat

RH – Fake sweep block; run fly route

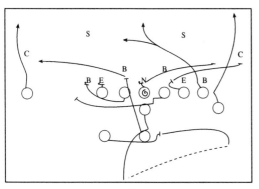

Vs. 5-0

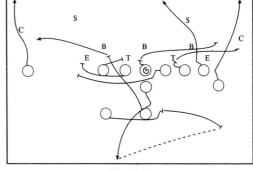

Vs. 4-3

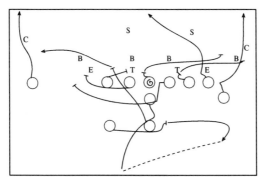

Vs. 4-4

PLAY #17: 121 WAGGLE OUT

Use vs. a soft corner or to take advantage of a mismatch with the spread end vs. their corner. (The fullback must gear down.)

Blocking Rules:

TE – Deep crossing route

RT – Pull; check 2

RG – Pull; read LG's block

OC – Block 1; cup right

LG – Pull; log end man

LT – Gap; down; on

SE – Out route

Backfield Coaching Points:

QB – Reverse pivot to midline; fake to LH; run pass option at flank

LH – Fake 21 sweep; block first man outside RT's block

FB – Dive for left foot on OC; block area; slide to flat

RH – Fake sweep block; run post route

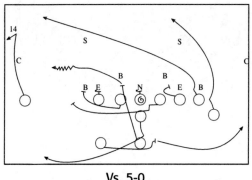

Vs. 5-0

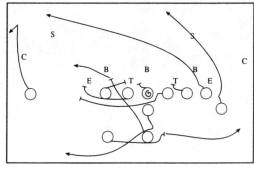

Vs. 4-3

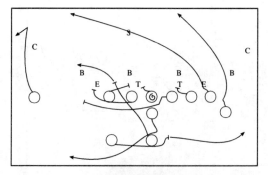

Vs. 4-4

PLAY #18: 121 WAGGLE CURL

Use vs. a corner using outside leverage to stop waggle out. (The fullback must stretch the underneath coverage.)

Blocking Rules:

TE – Post route

RT – Pull; check 2

RG – Pull; read LG's block

C – Block 1; cup right

LG – Pull; log end man

LT – Gap; down; on

SE – Curl Route

Backfield Coaching Points:

QB – Reverse pivot to midline; fake to LH; run pass option at flank

LH – Fake 21 sweep; block first man outside RT's block

FB – Dive for left foot of OC; block area; slide to flat

RH – Fake sweep block; run fly route

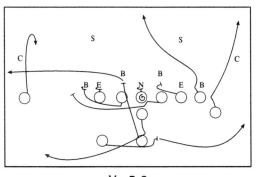

Vs. 5-0

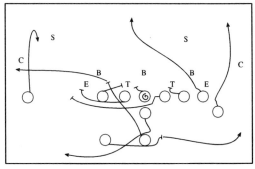

Vs. 4-3

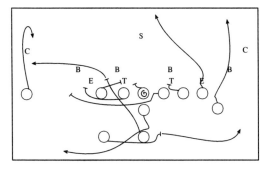

Vs. 4-4

PLAY #19: 121 WAGGLE WING AT 5

Use vs. a defense that is over compensating to stop the tight-end drag route. Also good vs. man-to-man coverage or two-deep coverage.

Blocking Rules:

TE – Fly route

RT – Pull; check 2

RG – Pull; read LG's block

C – Block 1; cup right

LG – Pull; log end man

LT – Gap; down; on

SE – Fly route

Backfield Coaching Points:

QB – Reverse pivot to midline; fake to LH; run pass option at flank

LH – Fake 21 sweep; block first man outside RT's block

FB – Dive for left foot of OC; block area; slide to flat

RH – Fake sweep block; start to run fly route, then run crossing route

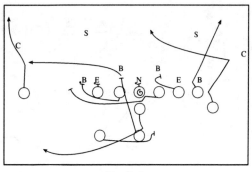

Vs. 5-0

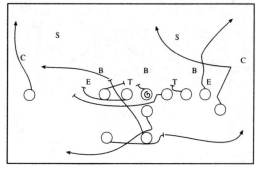

Vs. 4-3

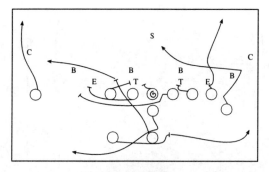

Vs. 4-4

PLAY #20: LOOSE STAR RED 29 WAGGLE WHEEL

Use vs. three deep coverage teams. (FB must gear down.) Do not run this play if the end man on the line of scrimmage is penetrating.

Blocking Rules:

TE – Curl route

RT – Gap; down; on

RG – Pull; log end man

OC – Block 1; cup left

LG – Pull; read RG's block

LT – Pull; check 2

SE – Wheel route

Backfield Coaching Points:

QB – Reverse pivot to midline; fake to LH; run pass option at flank

LH – Post route

FB – Dive for right foot of OC; block area; slide to flat

RH – 3-step motion; fake 29 sweep; block first man outside LT's block

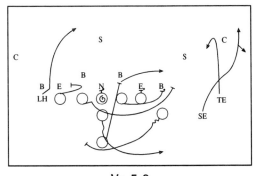

Vs. 5-0

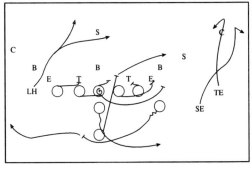

Vs. 4-3

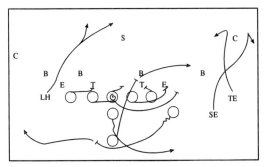

Vs. 4-4

PLAY #21: TIGHT 129 WAGGLE QUICK

Use on the goal line vs. eight-man front, penetrating defenses that also like man-to-man coverage.

Blocking Rules:

RE – Waggle route

RT – Gap; down, on

RG – Pull; log end man

C – On; left

LG – Pull; read RG's block

LT – Pull; check 2

LE – Crossing route

Backfield Coaching Points:

QB – Reverse pivot to midline; fake to RH; run pass option at the flank

LH – Dive for a point 1.5 yards outside end man; run fly route

FB – Dive for right foot of OC; cut block A gap defender

RH – 3-step motion; fake 29 sweep; block first man outside LT's block

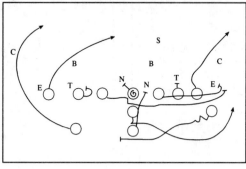

Vs. 6-2

We only run this play vs. goal-line defenses.

CHAPTER 2

THE

POWER SERIES

Run this power sweep when the linebackers are keying the offensive guards or when the defense is blitzing on the wing side. The zone blocking will pick up the blitzes.

Blocking Rules:

TE – Gap; post

RT – Fire on; backer

RG – Fire on; backer

C – Fire on; backer

LG – Fire on; backer
(pull; wall off with 6 call)

LT – Fire on; backer
(pull; check with 6 call)

SE – Out route

Backfield Coaching Points:

QB – Reverse pivot to midline;
hand off to LH; fake waggle

LH – Carrier; stay tight to RH's
down blocker

FB – Lead step; kick out first man
outside RH's block

RH – Block first free man inside

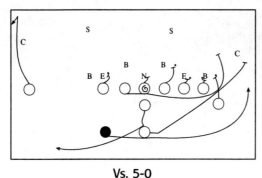

Vs. 5-0

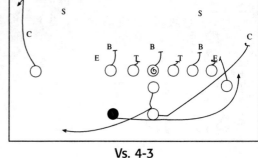

Vs. 4-3

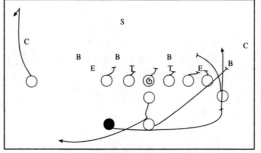

Vs. 4-4

PLAY #23: 132

Run this play in short-yardage situations when the end man on the line of scrimmage is penetrating to stop the sweep and the linebackers are keying the guards.

Blocking Rules:

TE – Lead; backer influence

RT – Gap; post, lead, backer

RG – Gap; area; post

C – On; left

LG – Pull; wall off

LT – Pull; check 2

SE – Out route

Backfield Coaching Points:

QB – Reverse pivot directly to
   LH; hand off; fake waggle

LH – Carrier; bend path for off–
   tackle area

FB – Kick out first man outside TE's
   block

RH – Influence end man on L.O.S.;
   block outside area

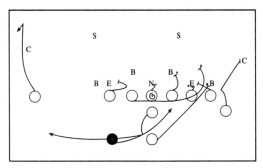

Vs. 5-0

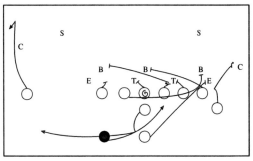

Vs. 4-3

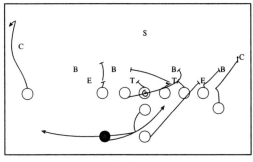

Vs. 4-4

PLAY #24: 134 BLAST

Run this play vs. a fast-flowing inside linebacker who is intent on getting outside to stop the sweep.

Blocking Rules:

TE – On; outside

RT – On; outside

RG – Gap; on; lead

C – On; left

LG – Pull; gut

LT – Fire on; backer

SE – Out route

Backfield Coaching Points:

QB – Reverse pivot directly to
    LH; hand off; fake waggle

LH – Carrier; stay tight to RG's
    block

FB – Lead step; block first backer
    from 5

RH – Cutoff

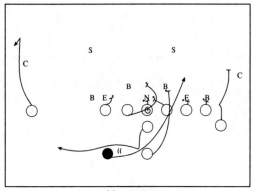

Vs. 5-0

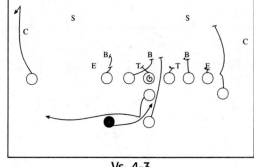

Vs. 4-3

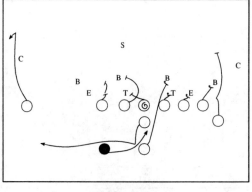

Vs. 4-4

PLAY #25: 137 COUNTER CRISS CROSS

Run this play when the defense is overpursuing the sweep. Also run this play when the end man on the line of scrimmage to the weakside is running upfield to stop the waggle.

Blocking Rules:

TE – Pull; wall off

RT – Pull; check 2

RG – Pull; trap

C – Post; right

LG – Post; lead backer

LT – Lead; backer; influence

SE – Stalk (crack if split)

Backfield Coaching Points:

QB – Reverse pivot directly to
  LH, hand off to LH, fake waggle

LH – Receive handoff; hand off to
  RH

FB – Kick out first man outside RT's
  block

RH – Carrier; take hand off from
  LH; bend path to LG's area

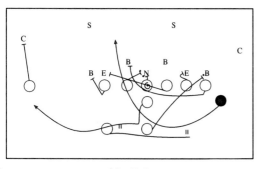

Vs. 5-0

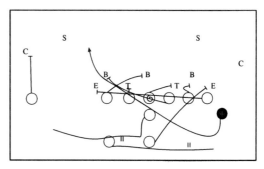

Vs. 4-3

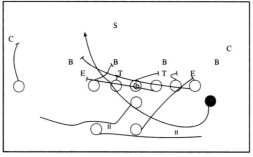

Vs. 4-4

PLAY #26: 137 COUNTER

Run this play for the same reasons for which a 137 Counter Criss Cross would be run. Because this play has only one hand off, it is safer and easier to execute.

Blocking Rules:

TE – Pull; wall off

RT – Pull; check 2

RG – Pull; trap

C – Post; right

LG – Post; lead; backer

LT – Lead; backer; influence

SE – Stalk (crack if split)

Backfield Coaching Points:

QB – Reverse pivot to midline; start downhill; hand off to RH; fake trap option

LH – Fake 61 trap option

FB – Kick out first man outside RT's block

RH – Carrier; bend path to LG's area

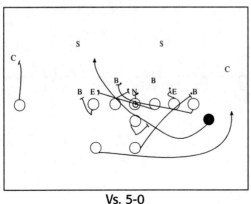

Vs. 5-0

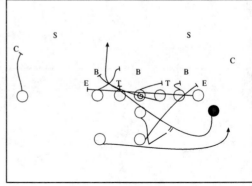

Vs. 4-3

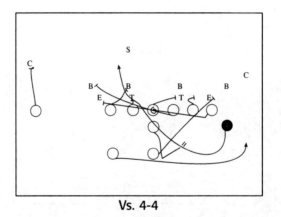

Vs. 4-4

CHAPTER 3

THE
TRAP OPTION
SERIES

PLAY #27: SPREAD 161 TRAP OPTION CRACK

Run this play when the defensive linemen are squeezing down with the offensive tackles to close down the trap play.

Blocking Rules:

SE – Crack 4

RT – Gap; bump lead; backer

RG – Gap; post; lead; backer

C – On; left

LG – Pull; log RT's area

LT – On; backer

TE – Cutoff

Backfield Coaching Points:

QB – Reverse pivot to midline; start downhill; option #3 for keep or pitch

LH – Run option path with QB

FB – Dive for left foot of OC; block area

RH – Flare, block 5

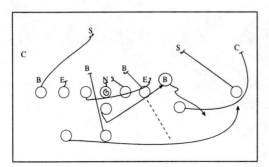

Vs. 5-0

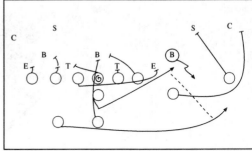

Vs. 4-3

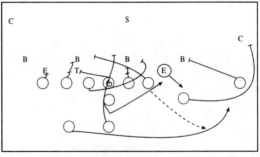

Vs. 4-4

PLAY #28: M SPREAD 161 TRAP OPTION CRACK

Run this play vs. a defense that likes to rotate with motion and for the same reasons the Spread 121 Trap Option Crack would be run.

Blocking Rules:

SE – Crack 4

RT – Gap; bump; lead; backer

RG – Gap; post; lead; backer

C – On; left

LG – Pull; log RT's area

LT – On; backer

TE – Cutoff

Backfield Coaching Points:

QB – Reverse pivot to midline; start downhill; option #3 for keep or pitch

LH – Run option path with QB

FB – Dive for left foot of OC; block area

RH – 3-step motion; reverse direction; block 5

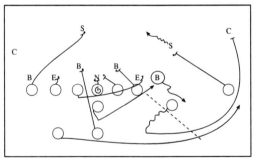

Vs. 5-0

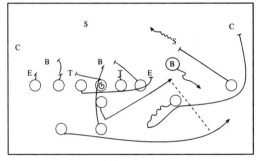

Vs. 4-3

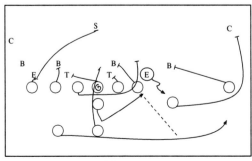

Vs. -4-4

PLAY #29: SPREAD 129

Run this play as a compliment to M spread 161 trap option. Run this play when the secondary rotates to the slot side and the end man on the line of scrimmage seals giving the lead halfback a chance to block him in.

Blocking Rules:

SE – Out route

RT – Cutoff

RG – Pull; wall off

C – Reach; area; away

LG – Pull; kick out

LT – Gap; read; down

TE – Gap; read; down

Backfield Coaching Points:

QB – Reverse pivot to midline; hand off to RH; fake waggle

LH – Go for a point 1.5 yards outside TE; block 1st free man inside

FB – Dive for right foot of OC; block area

RH – 3-step motion; carrier; stay tight to LH's block

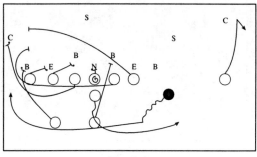

Vs. 5-0

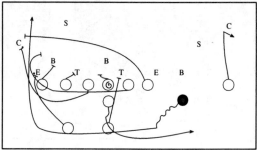

Vs. 4-3

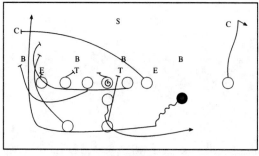

Vs. 4-4

PLAY #30: SPREAD 161 TRAP OPTION PASS

Use as a compliment to the trap option when the strong safety is reacting up to the L.O.S. quickly to beat the crack block.

Blocking Rules:

SE – Slant route

RT – Gap; on; area

RG – Gap; on; area

C – On; left

LG – Pull; block first man
  outside RT's block

LT – Step and cup

TE – Step and cup

Backfield Coaching Points:

QB – Reverse pivot to midline;
  start downhill; throw slant or
  flare

LH – Run option path with QB

FB – Dive for left foot of OC;
  block area

RH – Flare to outside leg of SE's;
  look for ball over inside shoulder

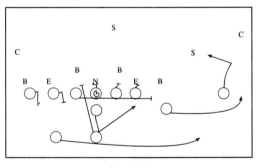

Vs. 5-0

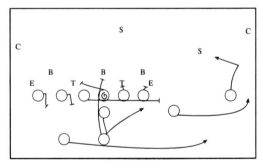

Vs. 4-3

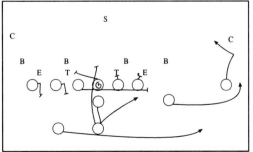

Vs. 4-4

PLAY #31: SPREAD 161 TRAP OPTION PASS FLOOD

Use this pass play to create a three-level stretch with the receivers. The QB should high-low stretch on the run-support defensive back.

Blocking Rules:

SE – Fly route

RT – Gap; on; area

RG – Gap; on; area

C – On; left

LG – Pull; block first man
   outside RT's block

LT – Step and cup

TE – Step and cup

Backfield Coaching Points:

QB – Reverse pivot to midline;
   start downhill; throw banana
   or flare

LH – Run option path with QB

FB – Dive for left foot of OC;
   block area

RH – Run banana route

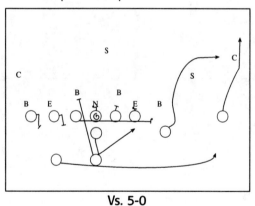
Vs. 5-0

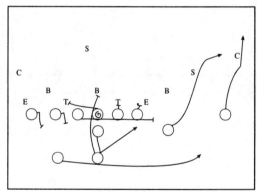
Vs. 4-3

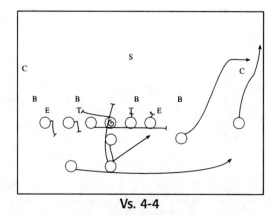
Vs. 4-4

PLAY #32: SLOT 161 TRAP OPTION PASS WHEEL

Use to create a three-level stretch with the receivers. The defender covering the flat should have a receiver in front and behind him.

Blocking Rules:

SE – Fly route

RT – Gap; on; area

RG – Gap; on; area

C – On; left

LG – Pull; block first man
    outside RT's block

LT – Step and cup

TE – Step and cup

Backfield Coaching Points:

QB – Reverse pivot to midline;
    start downhill; throw wheel or
    flare

LH – Run option path with QB

FB – Dive for left foot of OC;
    block area

RH – Run wheel route

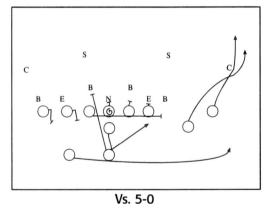

Vs. 5-0

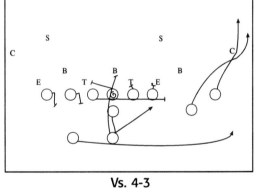

Vs. 4-3

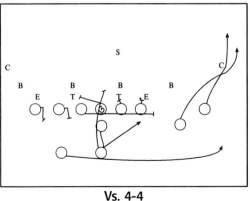

Vs. 4-4

PLAY #33: SPREAD 121 WAGGLE

Run this play as a compliment to the trap option. Use with a good running QB when the defense seals down with the tight end. Do not run this play when the end man on the line or scrimmage to the weakside is penetrating.

Blocking Rules:

TE – Waggle route

LT – Gap; down; on

LG – Pull; log end man

C – Block 1; cup right

RG – Pull; read LG's block

RT – Pull; check 2

SE – Post route

Backfield Coaching Points:

QB – Reverse pivot to midline; fake to LH; run pass option at the flank

LH – Fake 21 sweep; block first man outside RT's block

FB – Dive for left foot of OC; block area; slide to flat

RH – Run crossing route

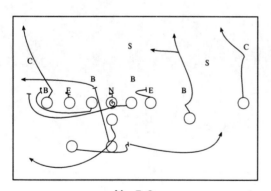

Vs. 5-0

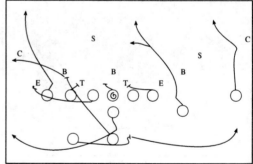

Vs. 4-3

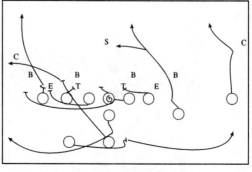

Vs. 4-4

PLAY #34: SPREAD 121 WAGGLE SHOVEL AT 8

Use vs. a defensive outside linebacker who is penetrating up the field to stop the quarterback running the waggle.

Blocking Rules:

TE – Lead; backer; influence

LT – Gap; post; lead; backer

LG – Area; post

C – On; right

RG – Pull; wall off

RT – Pull; check 2

SE – Cutoff

Backfield Coaching Points:

QB – Reverse pivot to midline; fake to LH; get depth; pitch to RH

LH – Fake 21 sweep; block first man outside RT's block

FB – Dive for left foot of OC; slide to flat; block corner

RH – Run to tail of LT; receive pitch; stay tight to TE's block

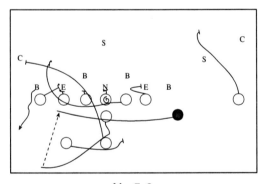

Vs. 5-0

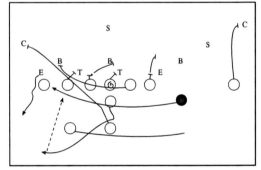

Vs. 4-3

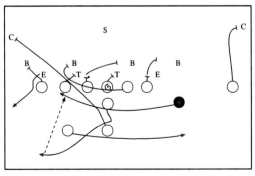

Vs. 4-4

PLAY #35: SLOT 121 WAGGLE AT 5

Use this play as a compliment to Trap Option Pass Wheel. Use vs. a defense that is overcompensating to stop the wing back on his drag route. Also good vs. man-to-man or two-deep coverage.

Blocking Rules:

TE – Waggle route

LT – Gap; down; on

LG – Pull; log end man

C – Block 1; cup right

RG – Pull; read LG's block

RT – Pull; check 2

SE – Run crossing route

Backfield Coaching Points:

QB – Reverse pivot to midline; fake to LH; run pass option at the flank

LH – Fake 21 sweep; block first man outside RT's block

FB – Dive for left foot of OC; block area; slide to flat

RH – Fake sweep block; run fly Route

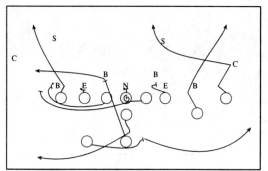

Vs. 5-0

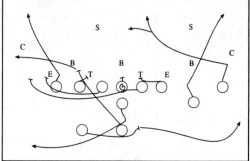

Vs. 4-3

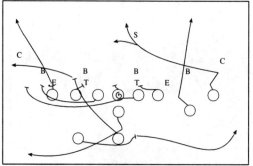

Vs. 4-4

PLAY #36: SPREAD 138 COUNTER CRISS CROSS

Run this play vs. a defense that overreacts to the trap option or sweep and also when the end man on the line of scrimmage is running upfield to stop the waggle.

Blocking Rules:

TE – Lead; backer; influence

LT – Gap; post; lead; backer

LG – Gap; area; post

C – On; right

RG – Pull; wall off

RT – Pull; check 2

SE – Cutoff

Backfield Coaching Points:

QB – Reverse pivot directly to LH; hand off to LH; fake waggle

LH – Receive hand off; hand off to RH

FB – Kick out first man outside RT's block

RH – Carrier; take hand off from LH; bend path for off-tackle area

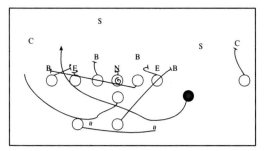

Vs. 5-0

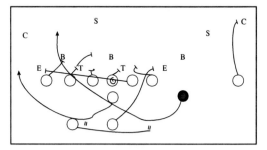

Vs. 4-3

Vs. 4-4

PLAY #37: SPREAD 161 TRAP OPTION REVERSE AT 9

Run this play in combination with spread 121 waggle or when the defense over reacts to the sweep and trap option. Do not run this play when the end man on the line of scrimmage to the weakside is running up the field to stop your waggle.

Blocking Rules:

TE – Waggle route; block 1/3

LT – Gap; down; on

LG – Pull right; reverse
  directions; log end man

C – Fire; on; backer

RG – Gap; on; backer

RT – Gap; on; backer

SE – Carrier; receive pitch;
  stay outside

Backfield Coaching Points:

QB – Reverse pivot to midline;
  start downhill; pitch to SE

LH – Run option path with QB

FB – Dive for left foot of OC;
  slide to flat; block area

RH – block first man outside RT's
  block

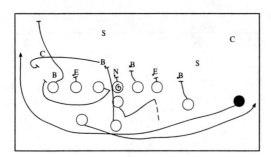

Vs. 5-0

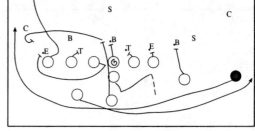

Vs. 4-3

Vs. 4-4

PLAY #38: SPREAD 161 TRAP OPTION REVERSE AT 9 PASS

Run this play for either the same reasons the trap option reverse would be run or if the corner is ignoring the tight end.

Blocking Rules:

TE – Waggle route

LT – Gap; down; on

LG – Pull right; reverse

    directions; log end man

C – Fire; on

RG – Gap; on; area

RT – Gap; on; area

SE – Receive pitch; throw to TE;

    stay outside

Backfield Coaching Points:

QB – Reverse pivot to midline;

    start downhill; pitch to SE

LH – Run option path with QB

FB – Dive for left foot of OC;

    block area; slide to flat

RH – block first man outside RT's

    block

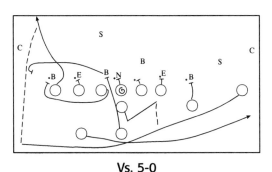

Vs. 5-0　　　　　　　　Vs. 4-3

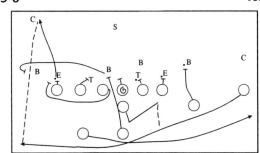

Vs. 4-4

PLAY #39: SPREAD 163 GUARD TRAP

Part of your trap option series, this is a play that enables you to trap the first man past the offensive guard instead of the first man past the offensive center like most guard traps. It should be run vs. even defenses and is best vs. an aggressive defensive end. The play becomes regular guard trap vs. a 5-0 defense.

Blocking Rules:

SE – Crack 4 or cutoff

RT – Gap; bump lead; backer

RG – Gap; post; lead; backer

C – On; left

LG – Pull; trap

LT – Fire on; backer

TE – On; backer; cutoff

Backfield Coaching Points:

QB – Reverse pivot beyond
    midline; hand off to FB;
    fake trap option

LH – Run option path with QB

FB – Dive for right foot of
    OC; carrier; stay tight to RT's block

RH – Flare; block corner or
    go to cutoff.

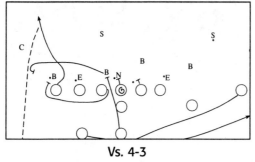

Vs. 4-3

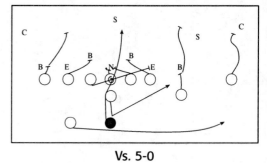

Vs. 5-0

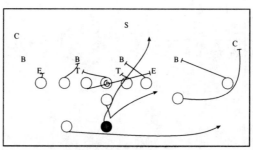

Vs. 4-4

PLAY #40: SPREAD 163 GUARD TRAP GUT

This play is also part of the trap option series. Run this play if the defensive end seals and stops the regular 23 guard trap.

Blocking Rules:

SE – Cutoff

RT – On; outside

RG – Gap; on lead

C – On; left

LG – Pull; gut

LT – Fire; on; backer

TE – On; backer; cutoff

Backfield Coaching Points:

QB – Reverse pivot beyond midline; hand off to FB; fake trap option

LH – Run option path with QB

FB – Dive for right foot of OC; carrier; stay tight to RG's block

RH – Block on; backer; cutoff

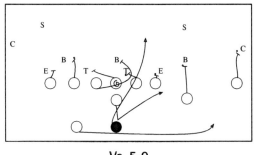

Vs. 5-0

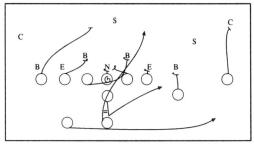

Vs. 4-3

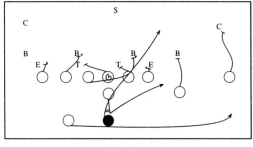

Vs. 4-4

PLAY #41: SPREAD 126 GUARD TRAP

This play is a compliment to M Spread 161 Trap Option. Run this play as part of the weak side sweep package from spread formation. Do not run this play if the defensive linemen are sealing down with the offensive tackle when he blocks down to the line.

Blocking Rules

TE – Backer; cutoff

LT – First backer from 5

LG – Lead; backer; influence

C – Post; right

RG – Pull; trap

RT – Block second man

SE – Out route

Backfield Coaching Points

QB – Reverse pivot to midline

    (over midline vs. odd); hand

    off to FB; fake waggle

LH – Dive for a point 1.5 yards

    outside TE; block at cutoff

FB – Dive for right foot of OC;

    carrier; stay tight to LG's block

RH – 3-step motion; fake 29

    sweep

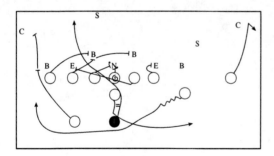

Vs. 5-0

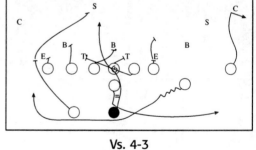

Vs. 4-3

Vs. 4-4

CHAPTER 4

THE
DOWN SERIES

PLAY #42: 182 DOWN

Run this play when the end man on the line of scrimmage is penetrating to stop the sweep or working out into the wing back.

Blocking Rules:

TE – Down; backer

RT – Gap; down; backer

RG – Pull; kick out

C – Fire on; backer

LG – Fire on; backer

LT – Fire on; backer

SE – Cutoff

Backfield Coaching Points:

QB – Reverse pivot flat down
    L.O.S.; hand off to FB; fake option

LH – 1-step motion; run option
    with QB

FB – Dive for outside foot of RT;
    carrier; stay tight to TE's block

RH – Block backer to cutoff

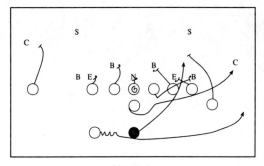

Vs. 5-0

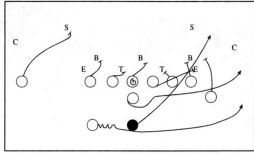

Vs. 4-3

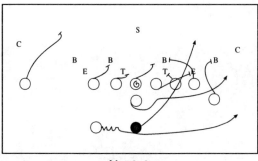

Vs. 4-4

PLAY #43: 182 GUT

Run this play when the end man on the line of scrimmage is penetrating or working out into the wing back. The pulling guard should wall off on the scraping inside linebacker.

Blocking Rules:

TE – Gap; down; backer

RT – Gap; down; backer

RG – Pull; gut

C – Fire on; backer

LG – Fire on; backer

LT – Fire on; backer

SE – Cutoff

Backfield Coaching Points:

QB – Reverse pivot flat down
L.O.S.; hand off to FB; fake option

LH – 1-step motion; run option
path with QB

FB – Dive for outside foot of RT;
carrier; stay tight to TE's block

RH – Block backer to cutoff

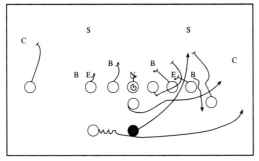

Vs. 5-0

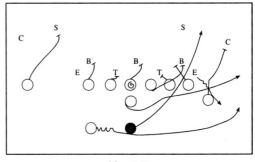

Vs. 4-3

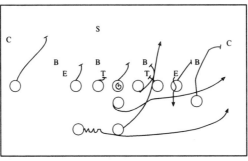

Vs. -4-4

PLAY #44: 182 DOWN OPTION

Run this play when the end man on the line or scrimmage is sealing down hard to stop 182 down. Do not run this play if the end man on the line of scrimmage is penetrating.

Blocking Rules

TE – Gap; down; backer

RT – Gap; down; backer

RG – Pull; log end man
   (wall off vs. 7 tech)

C – Fire on; backer

LG – Fire on; backer

LT – Fire on; backer

SE – Cutoff

Backfield Coaching Points

QB – Reverse pivot flat down
  L.O.S.; fake to FB; option #4
   for keep or pitch

LH – 1-step motion; run option
   path with QB

FB – Dive for outside foot of RT;
   take first opening to block the
   FS

RH– Block backer to cutoff

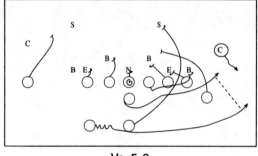

Vs. 5-0

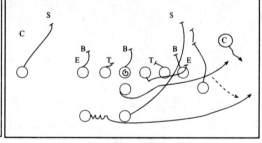

Vs. 4-3

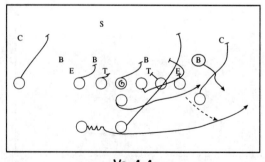

Vs. 4-4

PLAY #45: 182 DOWN LOAD

Run this play when the end man on the line of scrimmage is sealing and the halfback can block him physically. This will enable the guard to wall off on the scraping inside linebacker.

Blocking Rules:

TE – Gap; down; backer

RT – Gap; down; backer

RG – Pull; wall off

C – Fire on; backer

LG – Fire on; backer

LT – Fire on; backer

SE – Cutoff

Backfield Coaching Points:

QB – Reverse pivot flat down
  L.O.S.; fake to FB; option #4
  for keep or pitch

LH – 1-step motion; run option
  path with QB

FB – Dive for outside foot of RT;
  take first opening to block the FS

RH – Block first free man inside

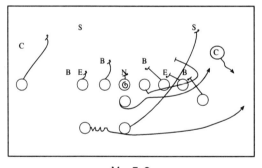

Vs. 5-0

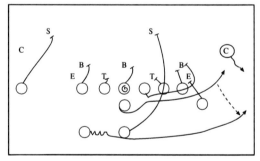

Vs. 4-3

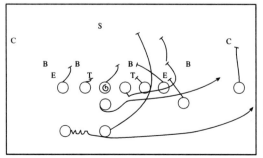

Vs. 4-4

Run this play from unbalanced.

PLAY #46: 183 CROSS BLOCK INFLUENCE

This play is the belly cross block to the tight end – wing back side. Run this against the eight-man front defense in combination with 181 keep pass.

Blocking Rules:

TE – First backer from 5

RT – Gap; down; on

RG – Gap; pull; kick out

C – Fire on; backer

LG – Fire on; backer

LT – Fire on; backer

SE – Cutoff

Backfield Coaching Points:

QB – Reverse pivot beyond
    midline; hand off to FB; fake
    keep pass

LH – 1-step motion; block first free
    man at the flank

FB – Carrier; lead step; bend path
    for inside foot of RT

RH – Influence end man on
    L.O.S.; block outside area

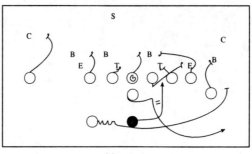

Vs. 4-4

We only run this play vs. a 4-4 defense.

PLAY #47: 181 KEEP PASS

Run this play vs. a corner who is quick to support the run vs. 82 down or 82 down option. Block solid if the defensive linemen are penetrating.

Blocking Rules:

TE – Seam route

RT – Gap; down

RG – Pull; log end man

C – Step and cup (fire vs. odd)

LG – Step and cup

LT – Step and cup

SE – Dig route

Backfield Coaching Points:

QB – Reverse pivot beyond midline; fake to FB; run pass option at the flank

LH – 1-step motion; block first free man at the flank

FB – Lead step; bend path for outside leg of RT; block area

RH – Run flat route

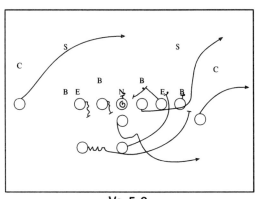

Vs. 5-0

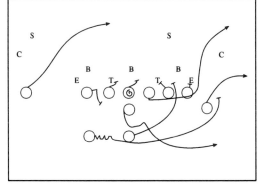

Vs. 4-3

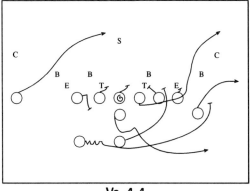

Vs. 4-4

PLAY #48: 181 KEEP PASS SWITCH

Run this play to soften the corner and change the routes at the point of attack from the base keep pass.

Blocking Rules:

TE – Flat route

RT – Gap; down

RG – Pull; log end man

C – Step and cup (fire vs. odd)

LG – Step and cup

LT – Step and cup

SE – Dig route

Backfield Coaching Points:

QB – Reverse pivot beyond
     midline; fake to FB; run pass
     option at the flank

LH – 1-step motion; block first free
     man at the flank

FB – Lead step; bend path for
     outside foot of RT; block area

RH – Run fly route

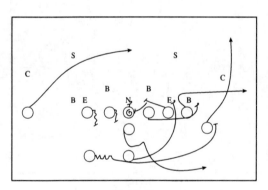

Vs. 5-0

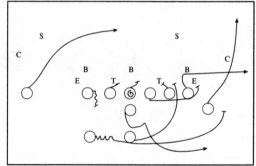

Vs. 4-3

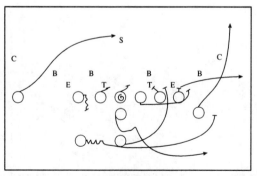

Vs. 4-4

PLAY #49: 183 PASS TE DRAG

Run this play in combination with 81 keep pass to attack the weak side of the coverage. The QB does not attack the flank, and the protection changes to turn back protection.

Blocking Rules	Backfield Coaching Points
TE – Drag route	QB – Reverse pivot beyond midline; fake to FB; pull up in G-T seam
RT – Gap; on; area outside	
RG – Gap; on; lead	
C – Post; left	LH – 1-step motion; block first man outside RT's block
LG – Step and fan	
LT – Step and fan	FB – Lead step; bend path for outside foot of RG; block area
SE – Dig route	
	RH – Run post route

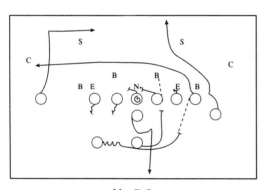

Vs. 5-0

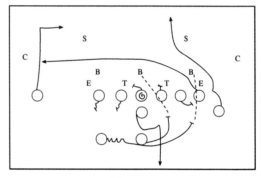

Vs. 4-3

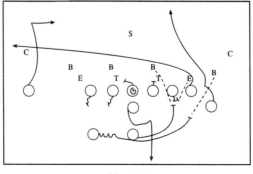

Vs. 4-4

PLAY #50: 181 KEEP PASS REVERSE AT 9

Run this play when the defense is over pursuing vs. 82 down, 82 down option, and 81 keep pass. This play should only be run when the end man on the line of scrimmage to the weakside is chasing flat from behind and trying to catch the QB from behind. Do not run this play if the end man on the line of scrimmage to the weakside is penetrating.

Blocking Rules:

TE – Seam route

RT – Gap; down

RG – Pull; log end man

C – Step and cup (fire vs. odd)

LG – Fire on; backer (peel)

LT – Fire on; backer (peel)

SE – Cutoff

Backfield Coaching Points:

QB – Reverse pivot beyond
  midline; hand off to RH; fake
  keep pass

LH – 1-step motion; block first free
  man at the flank

FB – Lead step; bend path for
  outside foot of RT; block area

RH – Carrier; crossover step;
  reverse directions; stay outside;
  peel block

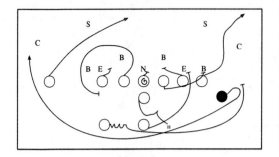

Vs. 5-0

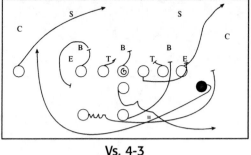

Vs. 4-3

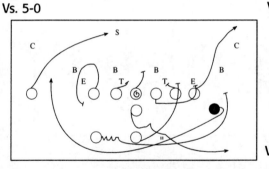

Vs. 4-4

PLAY #51: 187 COUNTER

Run this play when the linebackers are overpursuing to the strongside vs. 82 down, 82 down option, and 81 keep pass. This play involves the same blocking scheme as 137 counter criss cross.

Blocking Rules:

TE – Pull; wall off

RT – Pull; check 2

RG – Pull; trap

C – Post; right

LG – Post; lead; backer

LT – Lead; backer; influence

SE – Stalk (crack if split)

Backfield Coaching Points:

QB – Reverse pivot beyond midline; fake to FB; hand off to RH; fake keep pass

LH – 1-step motion; block first man at flank

FB – Lead step—bend path for outside foot of RT; block area

RH – Carrier, take hand off from QB; bend path to LG's area

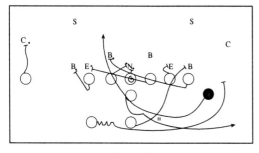

Vs. 5-0

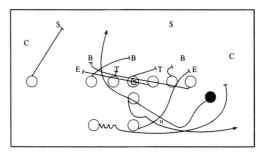

Vs. 4-3

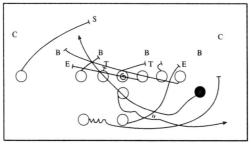

Vs. 4-4

PLAY #52: 181 WAGGLE

Run this play when the defense is over pursuing to stop 82 down, 82 down option, and 81 keep pass. Do not run this play if the defense likes to blitz their inside linebackers and do not run this play if the end man on the line of scrimmage to the weakside is penetrating.

Blocking Rules:

SE – Fly route

LT – Gap; down; on

LG – Pull; log end man

C – Block 1; cup right

RG – Pull; read LG's block

RT – Pull; check 2

TE – Crossing route

Backfield Coaching Points:

QB – Reverse pivot to midline; fake to LH; run pass option at flank

LH – 1-step motion; fake 81 keep pass; block first man outside Rt's block

FB – Lead step; dive for inside leg of RG; bend path to LG's area; slide to flat

RH – Run fly route

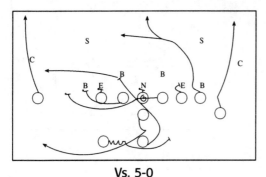

Vs. 5-0

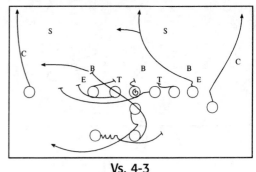

Vs. 4-3

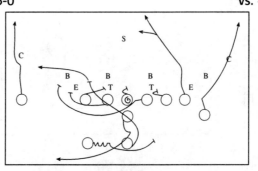

Vs. 4-4

CHAPTER 5

THE BELLY CROSS BLOCK SERIES

PLAY #53: 187 CROSS BLOCK

Run this play when the end man on the line of scrimmage to the weakside is penetrating to stop the waggle. The backside could be odd-blocked to insure a cut-back lane for the fullback.

Blocking Rules:

SE – Cutoff

LT – Gap; down; on

LG – Gap; pull; kick out

C – Fire on; backer

RG – Fire on; backer

RT – Fire on; backer

TE – Fire on; backer

Backfield Coaching Points:

QB – Reverse pivot beyond
   midline; hand off to FB; fake
   keep pass

LH – Jab step; dive for outside
   leg of LG; block first LB from 5

FB – Lead step; carrier; bend
   path for inside foot of LT

RH – 3-step motion; block first
   free man at flank

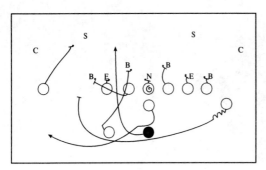

Vs. 5-0

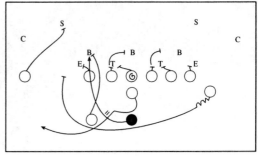

Vs. 4-3

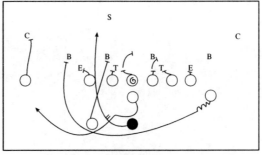

Vs. 4-4

PLAY #54: 187 ON

Run this play as opposed to 87 cross block vs. a three-linebacker defense. This play provides an opportunity to block all three fast flowing linebackers.

Blocking Rules:

SE – Cutoff

LT – On; outside

LG – Gap; on; backer

C – Fire on; backer

RG – Fire on; backer

RT – Fire on; backer

TE – Fire on; backer

Backfield Coaching Points:

QB – Reverse pivot beyond midline; hand off to FB; fake keep pass

LH – Dive for outside foot of LG; block first LB from 5

FB – Lead step; carrier; bend path for inside foot of LT

RH – 3-step motion; block first free man at flank

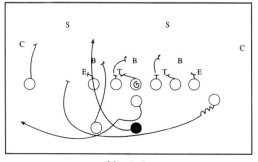

Vs. 5-0

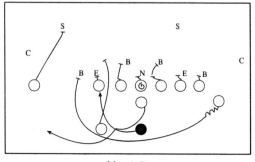

Vs. 4-3

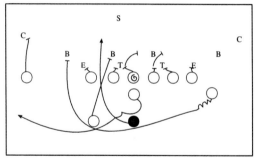

Vs. 4-4

PLAY #55: 189 KEEP PASS

Run this play as a run-pass option for the quarterback. Take the long completion if it is there or dump the ball off to the halfback in the flat quickly if the corner is soft. Do not run this play if the end man on the line of scrimmage to the weakside is penetrating.

Blocking Rules:

SE – Fly route

LT – Gap; down

LG – Pull; log end man

C – Step and cup (fire vs. odd)

RG – Step and cup

RT – Step and cup

TE – Step and cup

Backfield Coaching Points:

QB – Reverse pivot beyond
     midline; fake to FB; run pass
     option at flank

LH – Go for a point 1.5 yards
     outside LT; slide to flat

FB – Lead step; bend path for
     outside foot of LT; block area

RH – 3-step motion; block first free
     man at flank

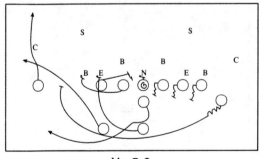

Vs. 5-0

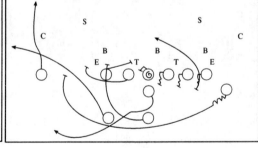

Vs. 4-3

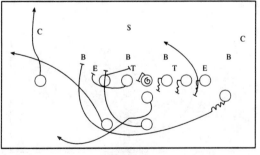

Vs. 4-4

PLAY #56: 189 WAGGLE

Run this play when the defense is overpursuing vs. the belly or the keep pass. Do not run this play when the end man on the line of scrimmage is penetrating or if the defense is blitzing their inside linebackers.

Blocking Rules:

TE – Waggle route

RT – Gap; down; on

RG – Pull; log end man

C – Block 1; cup left

LG – Pull; read RG's block

LT – Pull; check 2

SE – Post route

Backfield Coaching Points:

QB – Reverse pivot to midline; fake to RH; run pass option at flank

LH – Go for a point 1.5 yards outside LT; run crossing route

FB – Lead step; dive for inside leg of LG; bend path to RG's area; block area; slide to flat

RH – 3-step motion; fake 89 keep pass; block first free man outside LT's block

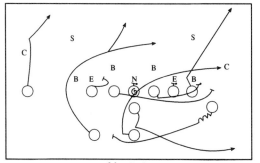

Vs. 5-0

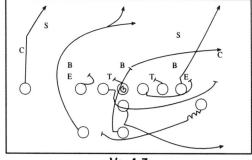

Vs. 4-3

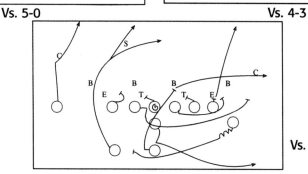

Vs. 4-4

PLAY #57: 134 COUNTER

Run this play when the defense is over pursuing to stop 87 cross block or 89 keep pass. Do not run this play if the defensive linemen are sealing down hard with the offensive tackles.

Blocking Rules:

TE – Backer; cutoff

RT – First backer from 5

RG – Lead; backer; influence

C – Post; lead; backer

LG – Area; post

LT – Pull; trap

SE – Cutoff

Backfield Coaching Points:

QB – Reverse pivot beyond
 midline; hand off to LH; fake
 bootleg

LH – Rock weight outside; carrier;
 bend path to near foot of OC

FB – Dive for outside foot of LG;
 block area

RH – 3-step motion; block first free
 man at flank

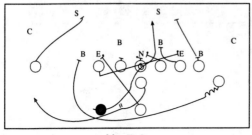

Vs. 5-0

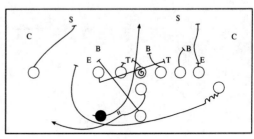

Vs. 4-3

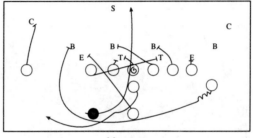

Vs. 4-4

PLAY #58: 134 COUNTER GUT

Run this play when the defensive linemen are sealing down hard to the inside when the offensive tackle blocks down. Also run this play when the defense is overpursuing to stop the belly or the keep pass.

Blocking Rules:

TE – Backer; cutoff

RT – Gap; on; backer

RG – Post; lead; backer

C – Post; lead; backer

LG – Area; post

LT – Pull; gut

SE – Cutoff

Backfield Coaching Points:

QB – Reverse pivot beyond midline; hand off to LH; fake bootleg

LH – Rock weight outside; carrier; bend path to near foot of OC

FB – Dive for outside leg of LG; block area

RH – 3-step motion; block first free man at flank

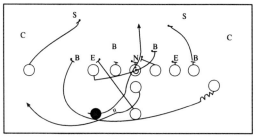

Vs. 5-0

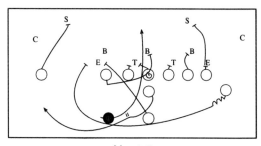

Vs. 4-3

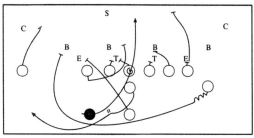

Vs. 4-4

PLAY #59: 134 COUNTER SPECIAL

Run this play vs. an aggressive pass rushing defensive lineman. Also run this play when the defense is overpursuing to stop the belly or the keep pass. Do not run this play vs. a defense that likes to blitz the inside linebackers.

Blocking Rules:

TE – First backer from 5

RT – Influence; block out

RG – Lead; backer; influence

C – Post; lead; backer

LG – Area; post

LT – Pull; trap

SE – Cutoff

Backfield Coaching Points:

QB – Reverse pivot beyond midline; hand off to LH; fake bootleg

LH – Rock weight outside; carrier; bend path to near foot of OC

FB – Dive for outside leg of LG; block area

RH – 3-step motion; block first free man at flank

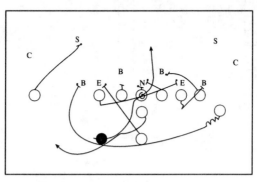

Vs. 5-0

PLAY #60 134 COUNTER AT 8

Run this play vs. a defense that overshifts to the tight end-wing back side. Run this play when the end man on the line of scrimmage to the weakside is penetrating. This play takes advantage of inside linebackers who are sitting inside, playing for the normal tackle trap counter.

Blocking Rules

SE – Cutoff

LT – Gap; post; lead; backer

LG – Gap; area; post

C – On; right

RG – Pull; wall off

RT – Pull; check 2

TE – Backer; cutoff

Backfield Coaching Points:

QB – Reverse pivot beyond
    midline; hand off to LH; fake
    bootleg

LH – Rock weight outside; carrier;
    bend path to outside leg of LT

FB – Dive for outside leg of LT;
    block end man

RH – 3-step motion; block first free
    man at flank

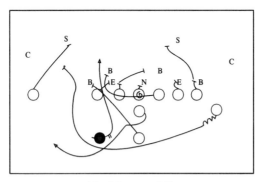

Vs. 50 overshift

PLAY #61: 134 COUNTER BOOTLEG

Run this play when the inside linebackers are sitting hard inside on the halfback who is running the counter play. Block solid on this play if the defensive linemen are penetrating. Do not run this play when the end man on the line of scrimmage to the weakside is penetrating.

Blocking Rules:

SE – Angle flag route

LT – Pull; block chase

LG – Area; post

C – Post; lead

RG – Gap; on; lead

RT – Gap; on; area

TE – Crossing route

Backfield Coaching Points:

QB – Reverse pivot beyond
    midline; fake to LH; run pass
    option at flank

LH – Rock weight outside; bend
    path to inside leg of LG; block
    area

FB – Dive for outside leg of LT;
    block area; slide to flat

RH – 3-step motion; block first free
    man at flank

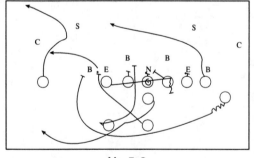

Vs. 5-0

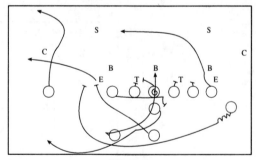

Vs. 4-3

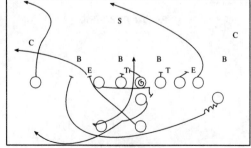

Vs. 4-4

PLAY #62: Z 182 DOWN

Run this play when the end man on the line of scrimmage penetrates when motion goes away from him. This is a good play to counter the wing-back motion. Do not run this play if the end man on the line of scrimmage is sealing down inside with the tight end.

Blocking Rules

TE – Down; backer

RT – Gap; down; backer

RG – Pull; trap

C – Fire on; backer

LG – Fire on; backer

LT – Fire on; backer

SE – Cutoff

Backfield Coaching Points:

QB – Reverse pivot flat down
   L.O.S.; hand off to FB; fake option

LH – Go for a point 1.5 yards
   outside LT; block area

FB – Dive for outside foot of RT;
   carrier; stay tight to TE's block

RH – 3-step motion; block first free
   man at flank

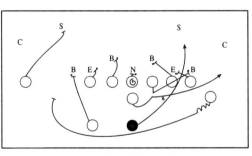

Vs. 5-0

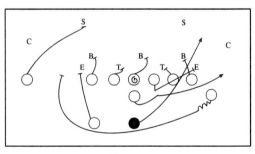

Vs. 4-3

We don't run this play vs. an eight-man front.

PLAY #63: 136 COUNTER LH DIVE

Run this play in combination with Z 182 down when the linebackers overreact to the down play. This is an especially good play vs. man-to-man coverage because the divide action in the backfield will split the two inside linebackers.

Blocking Rules

SE – Cut off

LT – First backer from 5

LG – Lead; backer; influence

C – Post; lead; backer

RG – Area; post

RT – Pull; trap

TE – Backer; cutoff

Backfield Coaching Points:

QB – Reverse pivot beyond midline; hand off to RH; fake bootleg

LH – Go for a point 1.5 yards outside LT; block area

FB – Dive for outside leg of RG; block area

RH – 3-step motion; carrier; bend path to near foot of OC

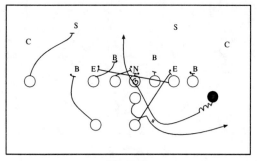

Vs. 5-0

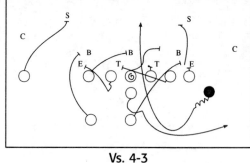

Vs. 4-3

Vs. 4-4

PLAY #64: 136 COUNTER BOOTLEG

Run this play when the linebackers are sitting hard inside on 136 counter. Block solid vs. a defensive line that likes to penetrate. Do not run this play if the end man on the line of scrimmage penetrates when the wing back motions away from him to stop the waggle.

Blocking Rules:

TE – Angle flag

RT – Pull; block chase

RG – Area; post

C – Post; lead

LG – Gap; on; lead

LT – Gap; on; lead

SE – Crossing route

Backfield Coaching Points:

QB – Reverse pivot beyond
  midline; fake to RH; run pass
  option at flank

LH – Block first free man at flank

FB – Dive for outside leg of RT;
  block area; slide to flat

RH – 3-step motion; bend path to
  inside leg of RG; block area

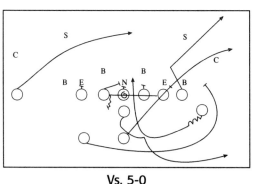

Vs. 5-0

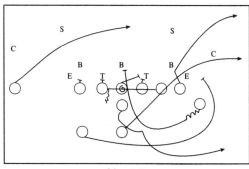

Vs. 4-3

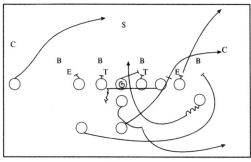

Vs. 4-4

PLAY #65: RIP 187 ISO

Runt this play vs. a three-linebacker defense when the defensive tackle playing inside the weakside offensive guard. This play provides extra blocking strength at the point of attack.

Blocking Rules:

SE – Cutoff

LT – On; outside

LG – Gap; on; lead

C – Fire on; backer

RG – Fire on; backer

RT – Fire on; backer

TE – Fire on; backer

Backfield Coaching Points:

QB – Reverse pivot beyond midline; hand off to FB; fake keep pass

LH – Dive for outside leg of LG; block first backer from 5

FB – Lead step; carrier; bend path for inside leg of LT

RH – Extended motion; turn up through inside leg of LT; block OLB

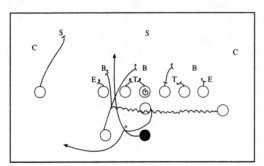

Vs. 4-3

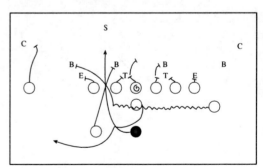

Vs. 4-4

PLAY #66: RIP 189 KEEP PASS FLOOD

Run this play when the objective is to flood the weakside with three receivers. Either look for the home run or high-low the flat coverage. Block the play with solid blocking if the defensive line penetrates.

Blocking Rules:

SE – Fly route

LT – Gap; down

LG – Pull; log end man

C – Step and cup (fire vs. odd)

RG – Step and cup

RT – Step and cup

TE – Step and cup

Backfield Coaching Points:

QB – Reverse pivot beyond midline; fake to FB; run pass option at flank

LH – Go for a point 1.5 yards outside LT; slide to flat

FB – Lead step; bend path to outside leg of LT; block area

RH – Extended motion; run banana route

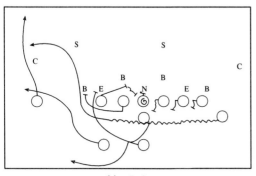

Vs. 5-0

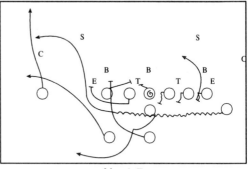

Vs. 4-3

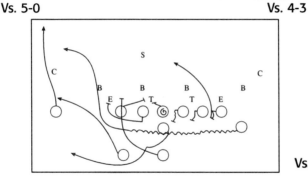

Vs. 4-4

PLAY #67: RIP 134 COUNTER

Run this play when the defense overpursues vs. the belly or the keep pass. Do not run this blocking scheme if the defensive line seals hard inside when the offensive tackle blocks down inside.

Blocking Rules:

TE – Backer; cutoff

RT – First backer from 5

RG – Lead; backer; influence

C – Post; lead; backer

LG – Area; post

LT – Pull; trap

SE – Cutoff

Backfield Coaching Points:

QB – Reverse pivot beyond
   midline; hand off to LH; fake
   bootleg

LH – Rock weight outside; carrier;
   bend path to near foot of OC

FB – Dive for outside leg of LG;
   block area

RH – Extended motion; block first
   free man outside LT's block

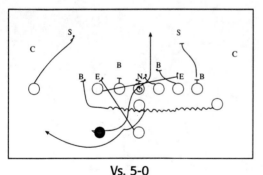

Vs. 5-0

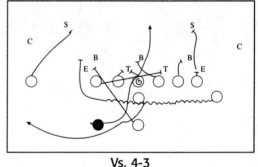

Vs. 4-3

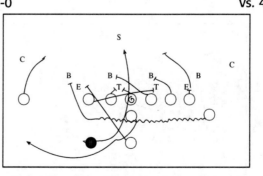

Vs. 4-4

PLAY #68: RIP 134 COUNTER BOOTLEG

Run this play when the defense is piling up the inside to stop the counter play, especially if the inside linebackers are holding inside on the counter. If the defensive linemen are penetrating, then the pulling tackle should block solid.

Blocking Rules:

SE – Angle flag route

LT – Pull; block chase

LG – Area; post

C – Post; lead

RG – Gap; on; lead

RT – Gap; on; area

TE – Crossing route

Backfield Coaching Points:

QB – Reverse pivot beyond
   midline; fake to LH; run pass
   option at flank

LH – Rock weight outside; bend
   path to inside leg of LG; block
   area

FB – Dive for outside leg of LT;
   block area; slide to flat

RH – Extended motion; block first
   free man at flank

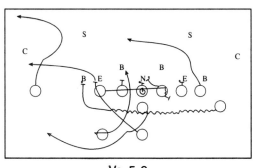

Vs. 5-0

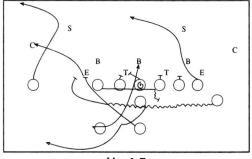

Vs. 4-3

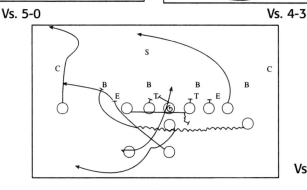

Vs. 4-4

PLAY #69: RIP 189 WAGGLE

Run this play when the defense is over pursuing against the belly and the keep pass. Do not run this play is the end man on the line of scrimmage is penetrating or if the defense is blitzing their inside linebackers.

Blocking Rules:

TE – Waggle route

RT – Gap; down; on

RG – Pull; log end man

C – Block 1; cup left

LG – Pull; read RG's block

LT – Pull; check 2

SE – Post route

Backfield Coaching Points:

QB – Reverse pivot to midline; fake to imaginary RH; run pass option at flank

LH – Go for a point 1.5 yards outside LT; run crossing route

FB – Lead step; dive for inside leg of LG; bend path to RG's area; block area; slide to flat

RH – Extended motion; run post route

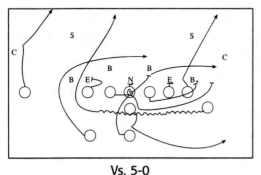

Vs. 5-0

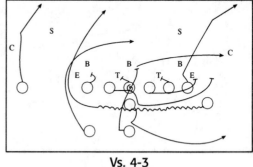

Vs. 4-3

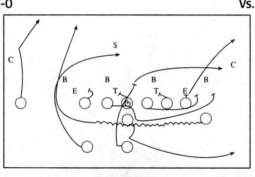

Vs. 4-4

PLAY #70: SPREAD 187 CROSS BLOCK RELEASE

Run this play with the tight end releasing outside to soften the outside line-backer. In addition, the backside guard and tackle could be odd-blocked to insure a cut-back seam for the fullback.

Blocking Rules:

TE – Outside release; cutoff corner

RT – Gap; down; on

RG – Gap; pull; kick out

C – Fire on; backer

LG – Fire on; backer

LT – Fire on; backer

SE – Cutoff

Backfield Coaching Points:

QB– Reverse pivot beyond midline; hand off to FB; fake keep pass

LH – Jab step; dive for outside leg of LG; block first LB from 5

FB – Lead step; carrier; bend path for inside foot of LT

RH – 3-step motion; block first free man at flank

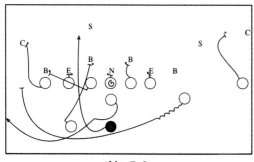

Vs. 5-0

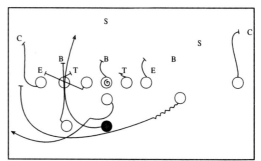

Vs. 4-3

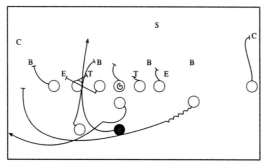

Vs. 4-4

PLAY #71: SPREAD 187 BLAST

Run this play to physically dominate a good nose guard. Do not run this play if the inside linebacker will mismatch your lead halfback or if the inside linebackers walk up tight on your offensive guards.

Blocking Rules:

TE – On; outside

LT – On; outside

LG – Gap; on; lead

C – Post; right

RG – Pull; wall off

RT – Gap; on; backer

SE – Cutoff

Backfield Coaching Points:

QB – Reverse pivot beyond
    midline; hand off to FB; fake
    keep pass

LH – Dive for outside leg of LG;
    block first backer from 5

FB – Lead step; carrier; bend
    path for inside leg of LT

RH – 3-step motion; block first free
    man at flank

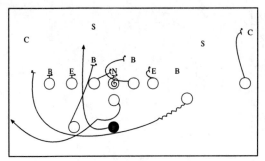

Vs. 5-0

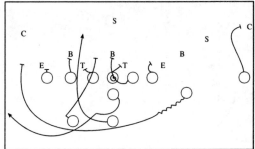

Vs. 4-3

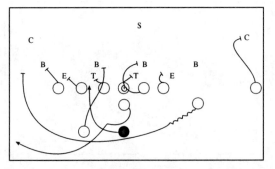

Vs. 4-4

PLAY #72: SPREAD 188 DOWN

Run this play when the end man on the line of scrimmage to the weakside is penetrating or is influenced by the path of the lead halfback. Do not run this play if the end man on the line of scrimmage is sealing down to stop the off tackle area.

Blocking Rules:

TE – Down; backer

LT – Gap; down; backer

LG – Pull; kick out

C – Fire on; backer

RG – Fire on; backer

RT – Fire on; backer

SE – Cutoff

Backfield Coaching Points:

QB – Reverse pivot flat down
L.O.S.; hand off to FB; fake option

LH – Go for a point 1.5 yards
outside TE; block backer to cutoff

FB – Dive for outside foot of LT;
carrier; stay tight to TE's block

RH – 3-step motion; run option
path with QB

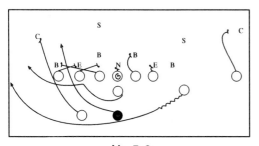

Vs. 5-0

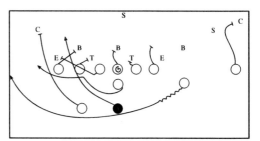

Vs. 4-3

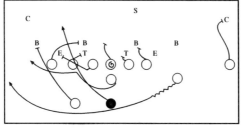

Vs. 4-4

PLAY #73: SPREAD 188 GUT

Run this play instead of spread 188 down when the end man on the line of scrimmage to the weakside is penetrating. This play will allow a team to wall off on a scraping inside linebacker.

Blocking Rules:

TE – Down; carrier

LT – Gap; down; backer

LG – Pull; gut

C – Fire on; backer

RG – Fire on; backer

RT – Fire on; backer

SE – Cutoff

Backfield Coaching Points:

QB – Reverse pivot flat down
  L.O.S.; hand off to FB; fake option

LH – Go for a point 1.5 yards
  outside TE; block backer to cutoff

FB – Dive for outside foot of LT;
  carrier; stay tight to TE's block

RH – 3-step motion; run option
  path with QB

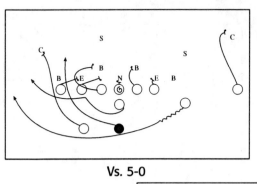

Vs. 5-0

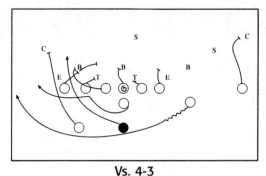

Vs. 4-3

Vs. 4-4

PLAY #74: SPREAD 188 DOWN OPTION

Run this play when the end man of the line of scrimmage is ignoring the load path of the lead halfback and sealing down inside to stop the off-tackle plays.

Blocking Rules:

TE – Gap; down; backer

LT – Gap; down; backer

LG – Pull; log end man
   (wall off vs. 7 tech.)

C – Fire on; backer

RG – Fire on; backer

RT – Fire on; backer

SE – Cutoff

Backfield Coaching Points:

QB – Reverse pivot flat down
   L.O.S.; fake to FB; option #4
   for keep or pitch

LH – Go for a point 1.5 yards
   outside TE; block backer to cutoff

FB – Dive for outside foot of LT;
   take first opening to block the FS

RH – 3-step motion; run option
   path with QB

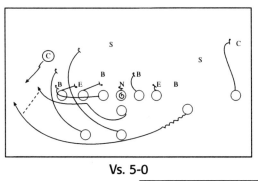

Vs. 5-0

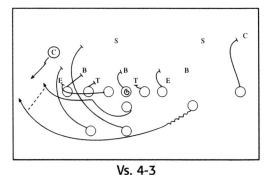

Vs. 4-3

Vs. 4-4

PLAY #75: SPREAD 189 KEEP PASS

Run this play when the defense is sitting hard inside on the fullback belly play. Do not run this play when the end man on the line of scrimmage to the weakside is penetrating.

Blocking Rules:

TE – Seam route

LT – Gap; down

LG – Pull; log end man

C – Step and cup (fire vs. odd)

RG – Step and cup

RT – Step and cup

SE – Dig route

Backfield Coaching Points:

QB – Reverse pivot beyond midline; fake to FB; run pass option at the flank

LH – Go for a point 1.5 yards outside TE; slide to flat

FB – Lead step; bend path for outside leg of LT; block area

RH – 3-step motion; block first free man at flank

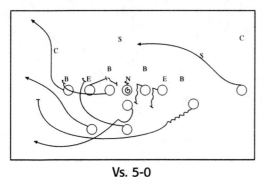

Vs. 5-0

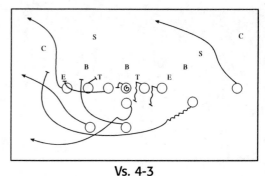

Vs. 4-3

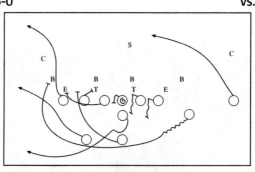

Vs. 4-4

PLAY #76: SPREAD 134 COUNTER

Run this play when the defense is overpursuing vs. the belly or the keep pass. Do not use this blocking scheme when the defensive linemen are sealing down hard inside when the offensive tackle blocks down inside.

Blocking Rules:

SE – Cutoff

RT – First backer from 5

RG – Lead; backer; influence

C – Post; lead; backer

LG – Area; post

LT – Pull; trap

TE – Cutoff

Backfield Coaching Points:

QB – Reverse pivot beyond midline; hand off to LH; fake bootleg

LH – Rock weight outside; carrier; bend path to near foot of OC

FB – Dive for outside leg of LG; block area

RH – 3-step motion; block first free man at flank

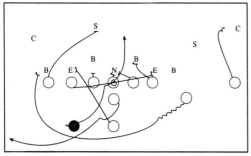

Vs. 5-0

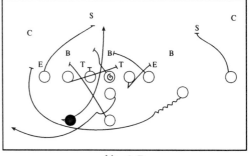

Vs. 4-3

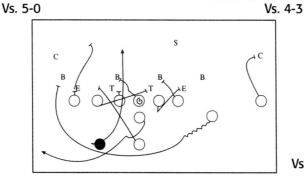

Vs. 4-4

PLAY #77: SPREAD 134 COUNTER BOOTLEG

Run this play when the defense is sitting hard inside on the counter play. Do not run this play when the end man on the line or scrimmage to the weakside is penetrating.

Blocking Rules:

TE – Angle flag route

LT – Pull; block chase

LG – Area; post

C – Post; lead

RG – Gap; on; area

RT – Gap; on; area

SE – Crossing route

Backfield Coaching Points:

QB – Reverse pivot beyond
   midline; fake to LH; run pass
   option at flank

LH – Rock weight outside; bend
   path to inside leg of LG; block
   area

FB – Dive for outside leg of LT;
   block area; slide to flat

RH – 3-step motion; block first free
   man at flank

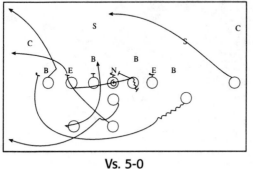

Vs. 5-0

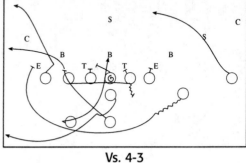

Vs. 4-3

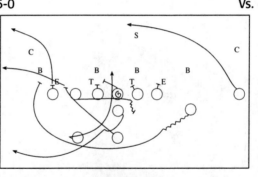

Vs. 4-4

PLAY #78: SPREAD 134 COUNTER AT 8

Run this play when the end man on the line of scrimmage to the weakside is penetrating to stop the weakside counter bootleg or sweep. Do not run this play when the end man on the line or scrimmage to the weakside is sealing down when the tight end blocks down inside.

Blocking Rules:

TE – Lead; backer; influence

LT – Gap; post; lead; backer

LG – Gap; area; post

C – On; right

RG – Pull; wall off

RT – Pull; check 2

SE – Cutoff

Backfield Coaching Points:

QB – Reverse pivot beyond midline; hand off to LH; fake bootleg

LH – Rock weight outside; carrier; bend path to outside leg of OC

FB – Dive for outside leg of LT; block end man

RH – 3-step motion; block first free man at flank

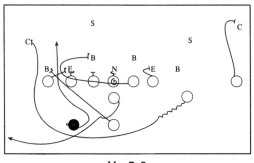

Vs. 5-0

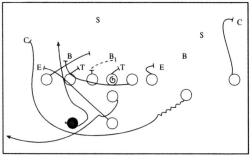

Vs. 4-3

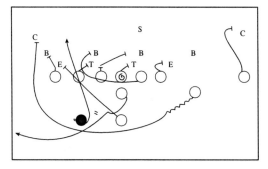

Vs. 4-4

PLAY #79: SPREAD 189 WAGGLE

Run this play when the defense is overpursuing vs. the belly to the weakside or the keep pass to the weakside. Do not run this play when the end man on the line of scrimmage is penetrating.

Blocking Rules:

SE – Fly route

RT – Gap; down; on

RG – Pull; log end man

C – Block 1; cup left

LG – Pull; read RG's block

LT – Pull; check 2

TE – Crossing route

Backfield Coaching Points:

QB – Reverse pivot to midline; fake to RH; run pass option at flank

LH – Go for a point 1.5 yards outside TE; run fly route

FB – Lead step; dive for inside leg of LG; bend path to RG's area; block area; slide to flat

RH – 3-step motion; fake 89 keep pass; block first man outside LT's block

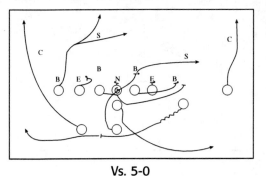

Vs. 5-0

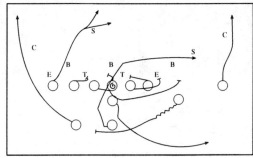

Vs. 4-3

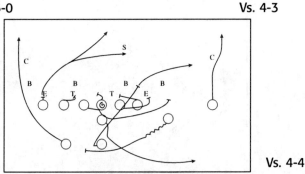

Vs. 4-4

PLAY #80: SPREAD 136 COUNTER LH DIVE

Run this play vs. scraping inside linebackers or when the linebackers are covering the backs man-to-man. The dividing action of the running backs will split the inside linebackers.

Blocking Rules:

TE – Backer; cutoff

LT – First backer from 5

LG – Lead; backer; influence

C – Post; lead; backer

RG – Area; post

RT – Pull; trap

SE – Cutoff

Backfield Coaching Points:

QB - Reverse pivot beyond midline; hand off to RH; fake bootleg

LH – Go for a point 1.5 yards outside TE; block at the cutoff

FB – Dive for outside leg of RG; block area

RH – 3-step motion; carrier; bend path for near foot of OC

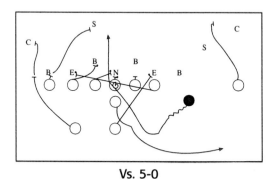

Vs. 5-0

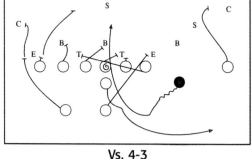

Vs. 4-3

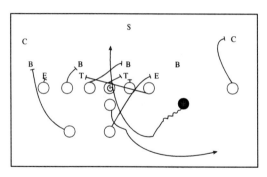

Vs. 4-4

PLAY #81: SPREAD 136 COUNTER BOOTLEG

Run this play when the defense is overpursuing vs. the belly or keep pass to the weakside. Also run this play when the inside linebackers are sitting hard inside on the counter play. Do not run this play when the end man on the line or scrimmage is penetrating. You could block solid if the defensive line is penetrating.

Blocking Rules:

SE – Angle flag

RT – Pull; block chase

RG – Area; post

C – Post; lead

LG – Gap; on; lead

LT – Gap; on; area

TE – Crossing route

Backfield Coaching Points:

QB – Reverse pivot beyond
    midline; fake to RH; run pass
    option at flank

LH – Block first free man at flank

FB – Dive for outside leg of RT;
    block area; slide to flat

RH – 3-step motion; bend path to
    inside leg of RG; block area

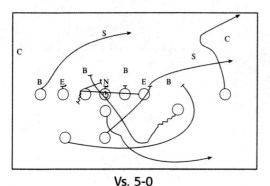

Vs. 5-0

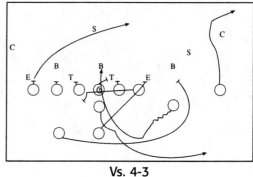

Vs. 4-3

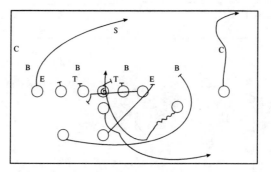

Vs. 4-4

PLAY #82: TIGHT 187 ON

Run this play in goal-line situations for a one-yard play. Do not run this play if the halfback is mismatched against the inside linebacker.

Blocking Rules:

LE – On; outside

LT – On; outside

LG – Gap; on; lead

C – Fire on; backer

RG – Fire on; backer

RT – Fire on; backer

RE – Fire on; backer

Backfield Coaching Points:

QB – Reverse pivot beyond midline; hand off to FB; fake keep pass

LH – Dive for outside leg of LG; block first backer from 5

FB – Lead step; carrier; bend path for inside foot of LT

RH – 3-step motion; block first free man at flank

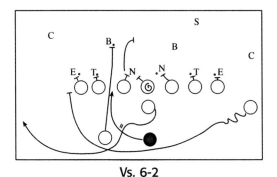

Vs. 6-2

We only run this play vs. goal-line defenses, but could run it against anything.

PLAY #83: TIGHT 189 KEEP PASS SOLID

Run this play in goal-line situations when the inside linebackers are stepping up hard inside on the belly play. Do not run this play when the end man on the line or scrimmage to the weakside is penetrating.

Blocking Rules:

LE – Seam route (inside release)

LT – Fire on; area

LG – Pull; log end man

C – Step and cup (fire vs. 6-2)

RG – Step and cup (fire vs. 6-2)

RT – Step and cup

RE – Step and cup

Backfield Coaching Points:

QB – Reverse pivot beyond midline; fake to FB; run pass option at flank

LH – Go for a point 1.5 yards outside TE; slide to flat

FB – Lead step; bend path to inside leg of LT; block area

RH – 3-step motion; block first free man at flank

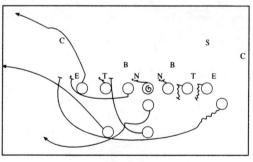

Vs. 6-2

We run this play only vs. goal line defenses but could run it against anything.

PLAY #84: TIGHT 134 COUNTER

Run this play in goal-line situations when the linebackers are overpursuing against the belly or belly keep pass and also when the defensive line is penetrating hard.

Blocking Rules:

RE – Backer; cutoff

RT – First backer from 5

RG – Lead; backer; influence

C – Post; lead; backer

LG – Area; post

LT – Pull; trap

LE – Cutoff

Backfield Coaching Points:

QB – Reverse pivot beyond midline; hand off to LH; fake bootleg

LH – Rock weight outside; carrier; bend path for inside leg of LG

FB – Dive for outside leg of LG; block area

RH – 3-step motion; block first free man at flank

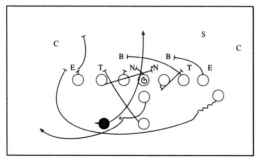

Vs. 6-2

We only run this play vs. goal line defenses, but could run it against anything.

PLAY #85: TIGHT 134 COUNTER BOOTLEG

Run this play in goal-line situations when the inside linebackers are sitting hard on the counter play. Do not run this play when the end man on the line of scrimmage to the weakside is penetrating. The line could also block this solid.

Blocking Rules:

LE – Angle flag route

LT – Pull; block chase

LG – Area; post

C – Post; lead

RG – Gap; on; lead

RT – Gap; on; area

RE – Crossing route

Backfield Coaching Points:

QB – Reverse pivot beyond midline; fake to LH; run pass option at flank

LH – Rock weight outside; bend path for inside leg of LG; block area

FB – Dive for outside leg of LT; block area; slide to flat

RH – 3-step motion; block first free man at flank

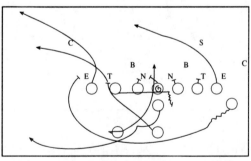

Vs. 6-2

We only run this play vs. goal-line defenses, but could run it against anything.

PLAY #86: TIGHT 136 COUNTER

Run this play in goal-line situations when the defensive line is penetrating and the linebackers are in man-to-man coverage. The split action by the running backs will divide the linebackers.

Blocking Rules:

LE – Backer; cutoff

LT – First backer from 5

LG – Lead; backer; influence

C – Post; lead; backer

RG – Area; post

RT – Pull; trap

RE – Cutoff

Backfield Coaching Points:

QB – Reverse pivot beyond
   midline; hand off to RH; fake
   bootleg

LH – Go for a point 1.5 yards
   outside LE; block first free man
   at flank

FB – Dive for outside leg of RG;
   block area

RH – 3-step motion; carrier; bend
   path for inside leg of RG

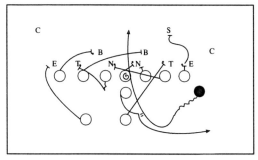

Vs. 6-2

We only run this play vs. goal line defenses but could run it against anything.

PLAY #87: TIGHT 136 COUNTER BOOTLEG

Run this play in goal-line situations when the linebackers are sitting hard inside to stop the counter play. The offensive line could also block this play solid. Do not run this play when the end man on the line of scrimmage is penetrating.

Blocking Rules:

RE – Angle flag route

RT – Pull; block chase

RG – Area; post

C – Post; lead

LG – Gap; on; lead

LT – Gap; on; area

LE – Crossing route

Backfield Coaching Points:

QB – Reverse pivot beyond
    midline; fake to RH; run pass
    option at flank

LH – Block first free man at flank

FB – Dive for outside leg of RG;
    block area; slide to flat

RH – 3-step motion; bend path
    for inside leg of RG; block area

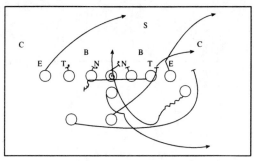

Vs. 6-2

We only run this play vs. goal-line defenses,
but could run it against anything.

PLAY #88: NO MO TIGHT 944 WEDGE

Run this play in goal-line situations for less than one yard. The halfbacks must get inside-out position on the first defenders to show outside the tight ends' blocks.

Blocking Rules:

RE – Gap on; backer

RT – Gap on; backer

RG – Gap on; backer

C – Fire on; backer

LG – Fire on; backer

LT – Fire on; backer

LE – Fire on; backer

Backfield Coaching Points:

QB – Open at 45 degrees to FB; hand off to FB; fake option

LH – Dive for inside foot of LE block first man outside LE's block

FB – Carrier; attack inside foot of RG; bend path to open area

RH – Dive for outside foot of RT; block first man outside RE's block

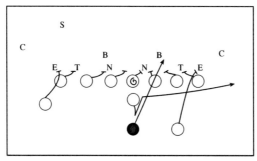

Vs. 6-2

We only run this play vs. goal-line defenses, but could run it against anything.

CHAPTER 6

THE
QUICK BELLY
SERIES

PLAY #89: SPREAD 184 (QUICK BELLY)

Run this play for a quick-hitting belly play to the split end-wing back side. This play makes the inside linebackers step up and sets up the quick belly option and the rest of the belly series.

Blocking Rules:

SE – Cutoff; corner

RT – Gap; on; backer

RG – Gap; on; backer

C – Fire on; backer

LG – Fire on; backer

LT – Fire on; backer

TE – Outside release; cutoff corner

Backfield Coaching Points:

QB – Jab step; reverse pivot
   hand off to FB; fake option

LH – 1-step motion; run option
   path with QB

FB – Lead step; carrier; attack
   outside leg of RG

RH – Flare; cutoff fourth defender

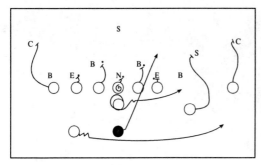

Vs. 5-0

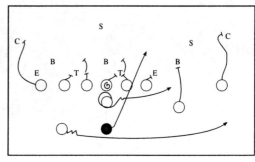

Vs. 4-3

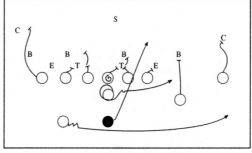

Vs. 4-4

PLAY #90: SPREAD 181 OPTION

Run this play when the inside linebackers are stepping up hard on the quick belly to the fullback.

Blocking Rules:

SE – Release; stalk 5

RT – Fire on; backer

RG – Fire on; backer

C – Fire on; backer

LG – Fire on; backer

LT – Fire on; backer

TE – Release; cutoff corner

Backfield Coaching Points:

QB – Jab step; reverse pivot fake to FB; keep or pitch off third defender

LH – 1-step motion; run option path with QB

FB – Lead step; dive for outside leg of RG; block area

RH – Flare release; stalk fourth defender

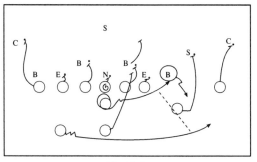

Vs. 5-0

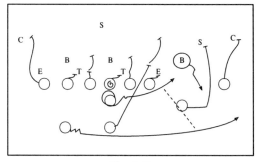

Vs. 4-3

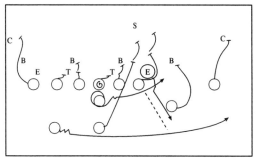

Vs. 4-4

PLAY #91: SPREAD 184 SCISSORS AT 6

Run this play when the defense is overpursuing vs. the quick belly and the quick belly option. Also run this play as a conflict for the play action passing game off the quick belly series.

Blocking Rules:

TE – Release cutoff; corner

LT – Outside

LG – Outside

C – Right gap; on; left

RG – On; area; delayed to backer

RT – Pull; gut

SE – Cutoff corner

Backfield Coaching Points:

QB – Jab step; reverse pivot
fake to FB; hand off to RH
fake option

LH – 1-step motion; run pitch path
with QB

FB – Lead step; dive for outside
leg of RG; block area

RH – Depth step; carrier; bend
path for tail of OC

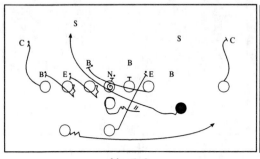

Vs. 5-0

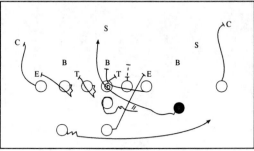

Vs. 4-3

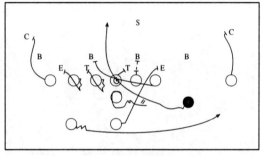

Vs. 4-4

PLAY #92: SPREAD 184 PASS

Run this play when the defensive backs overreact to the quick belly option. If the strong safety is quick to play the pitch on the option, then the halfback will get open behind him.

Blocking Rules:

SE – Fly route

RT – Gap; on; area; outside

RG – Gap; on; lead

C – Post; left

LG – Step and fan

LT – Step and fan

TE – Hook route

Backfield Coaching Points:

QB – Jab step; reverse pivot fake to FB; drop back five steps

LH – 1-step motion; fake 81 option; block first man outside RT's block

FB – Lead step; dive for outside leg of RG; block first backer from 5

RH – Run banana route

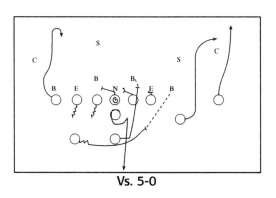

Vs. 5-0

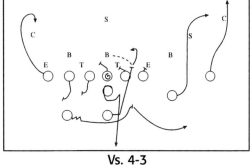

Vs. 4-3

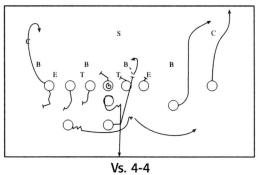

Vs. 4-4

PLAY #93: SPREAD 184 PASS SWITCH

Run this play when the defense stops spread 184 pass by keeping the corner in the deep third and hanging the strong safety under the banana route. Do not run this route vs. cover 2.

Blocking Rules:

SE – Out route

RT – Gap; on; area

RG – Gap; on; lead

C – Post; left

LG – Step and fan

LT – Step and fan

TE – Hook route

Backfield Coaching Points:

QB – Jab step; reverse pivot
fake to FB; drop back five steps

LH – 1-step motion; fake 81
option; block first man outside
RT's block

FB – Lead step; dive for outside
leg of RG; block first backer
from 5

RH – Run corner route

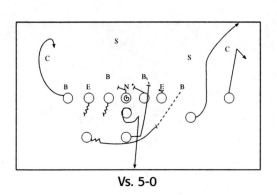

Vs. 5-0

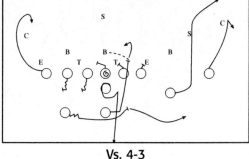

Vs. 4-3

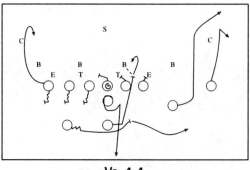

Vs. 4-4

PLAY #94: SPREAD 181 KEEP PASS

Run this play when the halfback can out leverage the strong safety in the flat, especially if the strong safety is quick to support the flank vs. the quick belly option.

Blocking Rules:	Backfield Coaching Points:

Blocking Rules:

SE – Fly route

RT – Gap; down

RG – Pull; log end man

C – Step and cup (fire vs. odd)

LG – Step and cup

LT – Step and cup

TE – Step and cup (delay)

Backfield Coaching Points:

QB – Reverse pivot beyond
   midline; fake to FB; run pass
   option at flank

LH – 1-step motion; block first free
   man at flank

FB – Lead step; bend path for
   outside leg of RT; block area

H – Run flat route

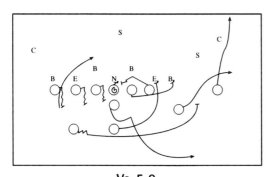

Vs. 5-0

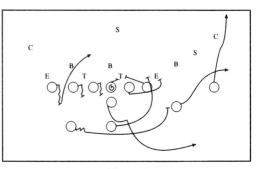

Vs. 4-3

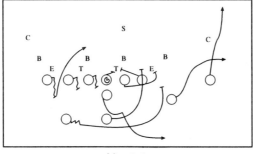

Vs. 4-4

PLAY #95: SPREAD 181 WAGGLE

Run this play when the defense is overpursuing vs. the quick belly or the belly option. Do not run this play when the end man on the line or scrimmage to the weakside is penetrating.

Blocking Rules:

TE – Waggle route (outside release)

LT – Gap; down; on

LG – Pull; log end man

C – Block 1; cup right

RG – Pull; read LG's block

RT – Pull; check 2

SE – Post route

Backfield Coaching Points:

QB – Reverse pivot to midline; fake to LH; run pass option at flank

LH – 1-step motion; fake 81 option; block first man outside RT's block

FB – Lead step; dive for inside leg of RG; bend path for LG; block area; slide to flat

RH – Run crossing route

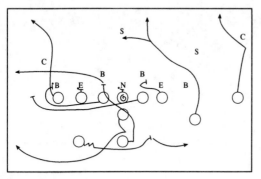

Vs. 5-0

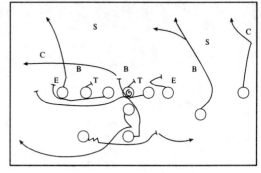

Vs. 4-3

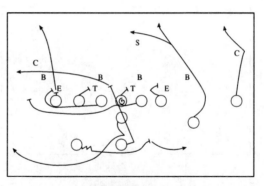

Vs. 4-4

PLAY #96: NO MO SPREAD 186 (QUICK BELLY)

Run this play to set up the weakside quick belly option package without motion. Run this play to make the linebackers step up which sets up, the weakside quick belly option.

Blocking Rules:

TE – Cutoff; corner (outside release)

LT – Gap; on; backer

LG – Gap; on; backer

C – Fire on; backer

RG – Fire on; backer

RT – Fire on; backer

SE – Cutoff corner

Backfield Coaching Points:

QB – Jab step; reverse pivot hand off to FB; fake option

LH – Rock weight outside; rock weight inside; run option path with QB

FB – Lead step; carrier; attack outside leg of LG

RH – Outside release; cutoff fourth defender

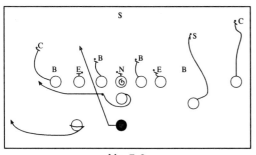

Vs. 5.0

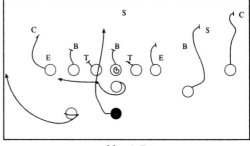

Vs. 4-3

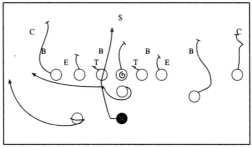

Vs. 4-4

PLAY #97: NO MO SPREAD 189 OPTION

Run this play when the defensive backs are rotating their coverage hard to the strength side. Also run this play when the inside linebackers are stepping up hard to stop the weakside quick belly.

Blocking Rules:

SE – Stalk corner (outside release)

RT – Fire on; backer

RG – Fire on; backer

C – Fire on; backer

LG – Fire on; backer

LT – Fire on; backer

TE – Cutoff corner

Backfield Coaching Points:

QB – Jab step; reverse pivot; fake to FB; keep or pitch off third defender

LH – Rock weight outside; rock weight inside; run option path with QB

FB – Lead step; dive for outside leg of LG; block area

RH – Flare release; cut off fourth defender

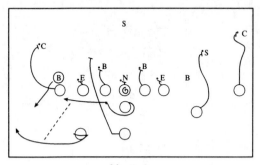

Vs. 5-0

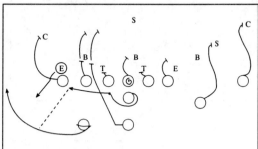

Vs. 4-3

PLAY #98: NO MO SPREAD 134 COUNTER

Run this play when the defense is over pursuing to the weakside to stop the weakside quick belly and the weakside quick belly option. Do not use this blocking scheme when the defensive linemen are sealing down hard inside when the offensive tackle blocks down inside.

Blocking Rules:

SE – Cutoff

RT – First backer from 5

RG – Lead; backer; influence

C – Post; lead; backer

LG – Area; post

LT – Pull; trap

TE – Backer; cutoff

Backfield Coaching Points:

QB – Reverse pivot beyond midline; hand off to LH; fake bootleg

LH – Rock weight outside; carrier; bend path for near foot of OC

FB – Dive for outside leg of LG; block area

RH – Flare release; cutoff fourth defender

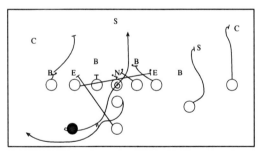

Vs. 5-0

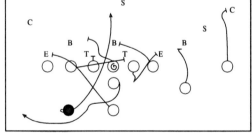

Vs. 4-3

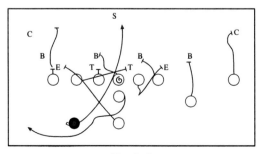

Vs. 4-4

PLAY #99: NO MO SPREAD 134 COUNTER AT 8

Run this play when the end man on the line of scrimmage to the weakside is penetrating. Also run this play when the inside linebackers are stepping up hard on the inside to stop the regular counter scheme.

Blocking Rules:

TE – Lead; backer; influence

LT – Gap; post; lead; backer

LG – Gap; area; post

C – On; right

RG – Pull; wall off

RT – Pull; check 2

SE – Cutoff corner

Backfield Coaching Points:

QB – Reverse pivot beyond
    midline; hand off to LH; fake
    bootleg

LH – Rock weight outside; carrier;
    bend path for outside foot of LT

FB – Dive for outside leg of LT;
    kick out first man outside TE's
    block

RH – Release outside; cut off fourth
    defender

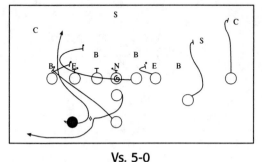

Vs. 5-0

Vs. 4-3

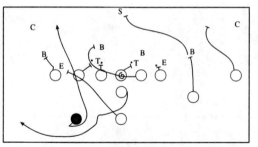

Vs. 4-4

PLAY #100: NO MO SPREAD 189 KEEP PASS

Run this play when the inside linebackers are stepping up hard to stop the quick belly or the counter and the weakside halfback can out leverage the coverage in the weakside flat. Do not run this play when the end man on the line of scrimmage to the weakside is penetrating.

Blocking Rules:

TE – Seam route

LT – Gap; down

LG – Pull; log end man

C – Step and cup (fire vs. odd)

RG – Step and cup

RT – Step and cup

SE – Post route

Backfield Coaching Points:

QB – Reverse pivot beyond midline; fake to FB; run pass option at flank

LH – Go for a point 1.5 yards outside TE; slide to flat

FB – Lead step; bend path to outside foot of LT; block area

RH – Outside release; run crossing route

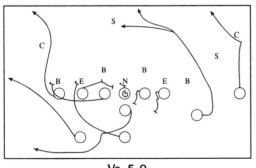

Vs. 5-0

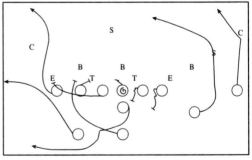

Vs. 4-3

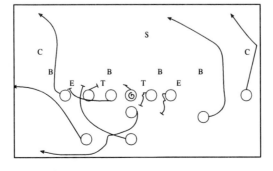

Vs. 4-4

PLAY #101: NO MO SPREAD 189 WAGGLE

Run this play when the defense is over pursuing to the weakside to stop the no mo option series. Do not run this play when the end man on the line of scrimmage is penetrating.

Blocking Rules:

SE – Fly route

RT – Gap; down; on

RG – Pull; log end man

C – Block 1; cup left

LG – Pull; read RG's block

LT – Pull; check 2

TE – Crossing route (outside release)

Backfield Coaching Points:

QB – Reverse pivot to midline; fake to imaginary RH; run pass option at flank

LH – Block first man outside LT's block; run fly route

FB – Lead step; dive for inside leg of LG; bend path to RG's area; block area; slide to flat

RH – Flare release; run banana route

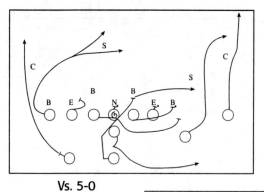

Vs. 5-0

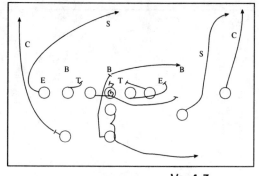

Vs. 4-3

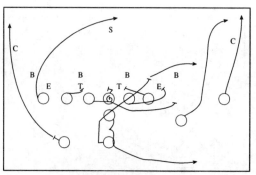

Vs. 4-4

Dennis Creehan is the special teams coordinator and the outside linebackers coach at Duke University. His three decades of coaching experience include successful stints at the high school, collegiate, and professional levels.

He began his coaching career (1971-74) at Keystone Oaks H.S. in Pittsburgh, Pennsylvania, after a stellar playing career as a strong safety at Edinboro University. A three-year starter for the Scots, Creehan served as team captain in his senior season, earned first-team all-ECAC accolades, and helped lead Edinboro to Lambert Bowl honors. At Keystone Oaks, he served as offensive and defensive coordinator and also coached wrestling and baseball.

In 1974, Creehan was the tight ends coach and recruiting coordinator for Johnny Majors at Pittsburgh. He then served as the offensive coordinator at Carnegie-Mellon for a single season, before returning to Edinboro for four years as defensive coordinator prior to the 1976 season. In 1980, Creehan was appointed head football coach at Edinboro, his alma mater. During his five years at the helm of the Scot's gridiron program, four of his teams were nationally ranked. For his efforts, he received three conference coach-of-the-year honors.

From 1985-to-1987 and 1991-to-1992, he was the defensive line coach and special teams coordinator for Edmonton Eskimos of the Canadian Football League. During his tenure with the Eskimos, Edmonton was 35-16, won two conference titles (1986, 1991), and appeared in the Grey Cup (1986). Then from 1987 to 1989, Creehan served as the outside linebackers coach at the University of California—Berkeley. Next, he moved to San Francisco State, when he was appointed the head football coach and assistant athletic director for the Gators.

In 1992, he returned to the head coaching ranks, when he was named head football coach at South Dakota. During his five years at the helm of the Coyotes, Creehan resuscitated a struggling program and led his teams to 28 wins, including 26 in his last three years at the helm. In 1997, Creehan moved to Arkansas State, where he served as defensive coordinator for a season, before assuming a position on the Rutger's staff for three seasons (1998-2000) as the defensive coordinator and outside linebacker coach.

Creehan is widely regarded as one of the most knowledgeable coaches in the game. He has authored a two-volume set of books on the wing-T offense, as well as developed a best-selling, 11-volume series of videos on the wing-T. In addition, Creehan is a very popular, well-respected speaker at coaching clinics across the United States.